PROPERTY INVESTMENT SUCCESS

HOW INVESTING IN THE PROPERTY MARKET CAN HELP SECURE YOUR FINANCIAL FUTURE

by Nick Fox

ISBN: 978-0-9576516-4-7

This book is not intended to provide personalised legal, financial or investment advice. Readers should seek professional advice with regard to such matters as interpretation of the law, proper accounting procedures, financial planning and tax before proceeding with any property investments. The Author and the Publisher specifically disclaim any liability, loss or risk which is incurred as a consequence, directly or indirectly, of the use and application of any contents of this work.

First published in England in 2014 by Fox Print Partners

PROPERTY

INVESTMENT

SUCCESS

HOW INVESTING IN THE PROPERTY MARKET CAN HELP SECURE YOUR FINANCIAL FUTURE

by Nick Fox

with Sarah Walker

published by Fox Print Partners

Contents

For my family, friends and business partners.
You all inspire me daily.
Thank you.

About the author

As is the case with so many successful businesspeople, Nick started young. When he was just ten years old, the mobile home he and his mother were living in burned down, all their belongings were lost and they were left with only the clothes they were wearing. Thankfully, the home had been insured and Nick's mother was able to buy a derelict Victorian terraced cottage. That was the moment Nick was thrown into the world of property.

Money was tight, so they had to do almost every bit of the renovation and refurbishment work themselves and young Nick quickly became an expert in stripping, plastering and painting. A couple of years later, the house was fixed up and had accrued a decent amount of equity, so Nick's mother sold it and put the money into a slightly larger property that also needed work – and so the process continued, moving them up the property ladder.

That was when Nick really began to understand not only what could be achieved by hard work, but also the potential of property as a money-making vehicle. He just needed a bit of capital to get him started.

He left school at 17 and tried his hand at a variety of temporary jobs, including bin man, warehouse packer and newspaper proofreader, but none really appealed. In 1988, at the age of 19, Nick landed a job with a company that imported computer software from America and sold it into retailers in the UK. It didn't take long for Nick to see the technology boom that was starting and he quickly realised he could do the same thing himself.

Operating out of his bedroom, Nick took out as many credit cards as he could and bought software stock from all over the world. He started off selling into small retailers, recycling his profits into more stock and the business expanded. As the market for personal computers really took off it was almost impossible to satisfy the demand. Nick moved his headquarters into a rented barn in the countryside, employed some staff, took on a business partner and grew the company until it became the UK's leading budget software company, selling over a million units every month into Dixons, Woolworths and WHSmith.

But by 2002, business had peaked. Now that the availability of technology had gone mainstream, with supermarkets sourcing stock directly themselves, nobody needed a middle-man and things quickly declined for Nick.

2005 was the turning point and a 'light bulb' moment for Nick, as he realised that the income he'd been getting from his various businesses had paid for a nice lifestyle, but it was his home that had built equity and given him a lump sum return. He knew that the quickest, and really the only way he could replace his financial losses was to buy more properties.

By the end of 2005, Nick had a portfolio of five properties, all rented to friends, which was generating an increasing amount of income for him and building equity at the same time. These first properties were apartments and small houses, all bought below market value, then Nick started buying larger homes, which he rented as single units to families. By the end of the following year, the portfolio had grown to 20 and Nick had a significant buy to let business.

In 2007, Nick went into a buying frenzy. Within 12 months, he'd added another 90 properties to his portfolio. Finance was easy to come by, other landlords were starting to offload part or all of their portfolios and, as Nick's reputation had grown in the area, he was getting a lot of deals through word of mouth, with agents sourcing bulk deals for him.

As the credit crunch hit and many of his mortgages moved off initial low fixed rates and onto variables, Nick started to look at how he could increase his profits and turned one of his existing family home lets into an HMO. That was light bulb moment number two.

Nick began to partner with other investors and subsequently doubled the size of his portfolio to more than 200 properties, around 100 of them HMOs. That portfolio is currently managed through the Milton Keynes letting agency he set up in 2010 and achieves 98% occupancy.

"Everyone thinks I must be constantly working to keep so many plates spinning but, really, I just employ great managers and develop effective systems."

For the past few years, Nick has been focused on consolidating his property business and sharing his knowledge and experience with other investors through mentoring. He also has business interests outside property: a photography business that he's looking to franchise nationwide and investment in a local pre-school that serves 80 children and has been rated 'outstanding' by OFSTED.

Nick loves football, tennis, golf and boating and has climbed Mount Snowdon with his partner, Samantha. He is committed to supporting local charitable causes and is also a Patron of Peace One Day. He and Samantha live just outside St Albans with their five children.

Author's disclaimer

I am not qualified to give financial or legal advice. All related recommendations made in this book should only be considered in consultation with suitably qualified and accredited professionals. Persons giving financial advice MUST be properly qualified and regulated by the Financial Services Authority (FSA) and anyone giving you legal advice should be suitably qualified and regulated by The Law Society and the Solicitors Regulation Authority (SRA) (or the Council of Licensed Conveyancers (CLC)).

Also by Nick Fox:

HMO Property Success

The Secrets of Buy to Let Success

Introduction

When I started working, I, like most people, was sold the benefits of investing in a pension plan: "The sooner you start, the better off you'll be in later life"... So I started paying into pensions and ISAs, because 'that's what you do'.

Then I watched as my father's pension provision came crashing down. During his working life, he was Financial Director for a number of major corporations and he'd been very well educated in the wisdom of investing in traditional pensions. But when the time came for him to commit to his annuity, the stock market was very low – not unlike it was in 2008/9 – and he found himself tied in to a very poor level of return. He was genuinely shocked at how bad his annuity purchasing power was. The expectation he'd had for his income in retirement – having paid in a considerable amount of money over the years – was not even close to what he would now realise.

When I started investing in property, my father saw the income returns I was making and used the capital he had not tied up in annuities to buy some properties himself. I manage those properties within my lettings portfolio and my father is now realising many times over the income he gets from the annuity payments he's receiving on a far greater amount of invested capital.

This is not a guide about how to invest for your pension; it's an overview of some of the options available to you, making the case for property as a sensible, reliable, flexible investment vehicle. I'm not trying to tell you where to put your money, just to open the discussion for you by looking at the realities, risks and rewards of investing in property versus going down the more traditional pension provision routes.

I hope you'll find what I have to say interesting and enlightening and that it will encourage you to at the very least think about your current financial provision; at most, to take the first step towards investment property success.

"More money has been made in real estate than in all industrial investments combined. The wise wage earner of today invests his money in real estate."

Andrew Carnegie

PART ONE:

SECURING YOUR FINANCIAL FUTURE

Chapter 1

What does financial security mean to you?

The concept of financial security is very personal. Your idea of the amount of money you would need and want in order to consider yourself financially 'secure' and your family properly provided for in the future, will be determined by your lifestyle, the size of your family, current financial commitments and future plans.

A lot of people talk about achieving 'financial freedom', but does that mean the same to you as financial security? Although it would undoubtedly be ideal to know that your investments would continue to deliver an excellent income while growing in capital value, without needing any day-to-day time commitment from you, would something less still give you security?

You might say that's all semantics, but my point is that you need to really think about what income and capital you're going to need for the rest of your life:

a. as a minimum, to ensure your financial commitments are covered and you can continue to have a good lifestyle, and

b. ideally – the amount that would allow you to live the life you dream of.

Once you've got those two figures – and it's going to take some time to work them out properly – then you can start to plot the steps you'll need to take to get there and set some measured, achievable goals that will enable you to build an investment portfolio that delivers on those goals.

Where are you now?

Far too many people have only a vague awareness of their own financial profile. I meet lots of budding investors who tell me they want to build a property portfolio for passive income so they can become financially free, but when I ask how much they need, why and by when, they have very little idea. All they really know is that they don't have enough right now and want more!

If you're really serious about having a financially secure future, you need to consult with an excellent wealth manager and/or financial advisor, and if they're going to advise you effectively, you've got to be able to give them an accurate picture of both where you are now and where you want to be. As I'll elaborate on in the next two chapters, one reason why pensions are failing to deliver is that many people simply haven't properly calculated what they're going to need in the future. And if you don't have a realistic target to aim for, you can't possibly expect everything to turn out 'fine'.

Set goals for yourself; if you don't know where you're going, how will you ever get there?

So, begin with your current lifestyle, financial and family situation, and put together a clear statement of your income and outgoings every month and year. I use Excel to keep a clear track of my assets, other investments, monthly income and expenditure, plus a budget, which I revise every month. However you choose to collate this information, your 'financial statement' should include:

- Monthly income & expenditure, remembering:
  - the spread cost of any one-off or lump-sum annual
  - outgoings, such as Christmas, car servicing and holidays
  - Allowances for eating out and entertaining
  - Income from investments – you may need to put this down as average estimates
- Information on existing property assets - borrowing, interest rate, term of loan, repayment amount, cash flow, etc.
- Details of any other investments
- Your current pension provision (see Chapter 2)
- Credit card and loan rates & outstanding balances
- Any other assets
- All on-going financial commitments, such as school fees.

It's important to be realistic about your expenditure. This exercise is the first step towards establishing how much income you'll need in retirement, so be absolutely honest about how much you spend – and on what.

What do you need and want?

You can fine-tune your projections when you meet with your advisor, but it's important that you have a clear plan to discuss with them. And remember that your future begins right away - it's not just about retirement - so make plans and calculations relating to the short, medium and long term.

If you've never put pen to paper regarding financial and lifestyle goals, I'd recommend you read 'Goals' by Brian Tracy and 'Goal Mapping' by Brian Mayne. There's a skill to doing it right, much of which comes down to managing your time excellently and committing to doing what you've said you'll do – and neither of those things are as easy as you might think! The vast majority of people need to train themselves to be disciplined and a very big help in succeeding with this is having someone that you make yourself accountable to. It's a bit like sticking to new years' resolutions or diets – telling someone else what you're doing and asking them to keep checking up on you is a great motivator for staying on track.

The other thing that will really help is having a visual representation of what you're trying to achieve. We subconsciously focus on the things we see and hear most often, so when you've got your goals down in black & white, stick some of the key figures, targets and end-game images around your home and office. I've done this for a number of years now and I promise you, it works. Some people talk about having a vision board; I have lots of them, from A5 size on the fridge, to big panels - several feet wide - in my office. That may be a bit extreme for you (!), but do make sure you have some kind of visual reminders of your targets for the short, medium and long-term and something that represents the kind of life you want in retirement.

So, on to your projections. I'd recommend that, using the calculations and information you put together for your financial statement, look at how much income is required to cover all your expenses, and estimate the figures for different timeframes, e.g.

- Over the next couple of years
- In, say, 5 years, when one or more children might be at secondary school
- In 10 years, when you are mortgage-free, but your children are at university and when you perhaps might want to remodel or update your home
- In 15 years, when all your children have left home
- In 20 years.

Include absolutely everything that would allow you to continue to live your current lifestyle, plus a 10% contingency.

Then add in the things that you don't do at the moment, but would like to be able to, for example: additional travel and holidays; investments and provision you might want to make for your children or other family members, perhaps deposits for homes or putting money into trusts; charitable contributions, and new assets and personal items you might want to buy, such as cars, jewellery, art and clothes.

This should highlight the kind of money you'll need and when you'll need it in order to live the life you want – both in terms of on-going income and lump sum capital returns.

Consult with the best advisors you can find

Now that you have your personal financial statement and your short, medium and long-term needs and plans drafted out, you're in the right position to get professional financial advice. Having all this information to hand means that when you meet with advisors, you can make the best use of the time you're paying for – and they'll be very grateful to have such an organised client! They will be able to help you calculate the kind of savings and investments you'll need to make in order to achieve the income and level of financial security you want.

Note that all professionals giving you financial advice MUST be properly qualified and regulated by the Financial Services Authority (FSA).

The first financial professional you should engage is a Wealth Manager. They will look at all your financial affairs – mortgages, savings, investments, earnings, and so on – essentially as a portfolio, within the context of your business, lifestyle, family situation and desires for the future. They'll be able to advise you on the kinds of investment you should consider in order to achieve the right returns, in the most tax-efficient way. If you can find a Wealth Manager who invests in property themselves, that would be ideal.

Wealth Managers should also have the CISI Masters in Wealth Management (MCSI after their name).

Assuming that when you've finished reading this book you're still seriously considering investing in property, you should also engage an independent mortgage broker, who has plenty of experience in securing buy to let mortgages, and a property tax specialist. You may already have an accountant, and your wealth manager will certainly be able to give you tax advice, but property tax is quite complex and you need someone who knows what allowances you can take advantage of, when and from where. Make sure they're happy to liaise with your wealth manager, so that you get an accurate picture of how income and gains from various property investments might impact your overall tax position.

Any person acting as a broker or making recommendations for your mortgage finance must have one or more of these qualifications: Certificate in Mortgage Advice (Cert MA); Certificate in Mortgage

Advice and Practice (CeMAP) from the ifa School of Finance; Mortgage Advice and Practice Certificate (MAPC) from the CIB in Scotland.

As well as qualifying under the Association of Chartered Certified Accountants (ACCA), your tax advisor should also be a member of the Chartered Institute of Taxation (CTA).

Clients often ask if I can recommend advisors to them. Mine are excellent and I'm happy to disclose who they are, but I do recommend you find someone reasonably local to you, as face-to-face meetings are always the most beneficial and you don't want to have to travel long distances every time you meet, or when you need to exchange paperwork.

Ask friends, family and colleagues for their experiences and recommendations with regard to wealth advisors in your local area, then make appointments with them in order to see who you feel is going to be the best fit for you and your financial plans. Building your own 'power team' of specialists is very important.

KEY NOTES

- Put together a complete 'statement' detailing your current financial position: income & expenditure, assets & liabilities, investments

- Research goal-setting techniques

- Project your lifestyle and financial requirements for the short, medium and long-term future

- Get an idea of what financial security would mean for you

- Meet with a Wealth Manager

Chapter 2

The problem(s) with pensions

Savers are being left thousands of pounds worse off in retirement because of a "broken" pensions market. Insurance firms are not encouraging customers to shop around for the best deal, and are making a "significant" extra profit as a result.'

The Telegraph, February 2014

For the last few years, pensions have been at the forefront of the financial headlines: concerns over shortfalls in final salary schemes and investment funds not maturing as originally anticipated; fraud; fees being excessive; annuities being mis-sold – and so it goes on.

As I write, the Association of British Insurers and its members are in the process of carrying out an audit of older pension schemes, overseen by an independent panel. The fact that this audit has been commissioned is an admission by the industry that, for far too long, pension schemes have been flawed and an acknowledgment that something needs to be done to improve the situation of those whose investments are unlikely to mature at an adequate level.

Your current pension provision

Channel 4's 'Dispatches' programme reported in November 2013, 'Most people can't actually tell you exactly what they've invested in their pension, how funds are performing or how it's likely to mature. They're paying in blindly.' Not only that, but far too many people have no idea how much they're even going to need in retirement. The programme calculated that to have just £15,000 income in retirement today, you need to have saved £150,000 to top up the state pension, and a child born today will need to have saved around £2.4 million in order to have a 'comfortable' retirement.

So how does your current pension provision look?

If you've simply paid into a standard workplace pension and/or have taken an annuity offered by your provider without shopping around, I'd go so far as to say there's no chance it will mature to give you anywhere near the income you'll need – never mind *want* – for a 'comfortable' retirement.

Basic workplace pensions are linked to your salary and we also tend to invest into private pensions based on a percentage of what we bring home. But with wages not rising in line with inflation and life expectancy increasing, have you reassessed how your pension is likely to mature? If you haven't, make sure your Wealth Manager or IFA takes a look and explains to you how much you can expect to receive, based on their projections.

The reason I've chosen to put most of my pension provision eggs in the property basket, rather than into 'traditional' pension schemes is because I believe – as does the Financial Conduct Authority, according to the headlines – that the UK pension system is 'not working' (BBC, February 2014). I think there are fundamental issues with the schemes on offer, particularly annuities, and I don't want to leave my financial future in the hands of strangers managing what I see as very mediocre funds.

But before I go on to annuities and funds in more detail, I just want to stress the importance of understanding your pension – both the options that are available to you and your own needs for retirement.

You may have noticed there's been a lot of talk over the past year about the new legislation regarding workplace pensions. The fact that all employers must enrol their employees in a pension scheme might sound good, but the amount paid in could be so low that the end provision could still be massively inadequate. Two million people were automatically enrolled in a workplace pension scheme in 2013, but I wonder how many of them have bothered to calculate either how the pension will mature or what percentage of their required income in retirement it will actually represent? There is a danger that insisting on workplace pensions could be doing savers a disservice, causing them to think their pension has now been taken care of and that they don't need to worry any more.

So if you haven't already sat down and done the 'financial statement' exercise in Chapter 1, do it now. You simply cannot afford to have the wrong impression about the shape of your finances or your future needs.

Fundamental problems with annuities

Most people's pension provision is based on their having taken out an annuity - essentially an insurance policy that pays out in retirement. The biggest 'scandal' here, for me, is the fact that single-life annuities – the ones that are sold as 'standard' – die with you. You pay into your pension fund every month so that you will be guaranteed a certain level of income from the fund after you retire, but on your death, regardless of when that occurs, your fund essentially ceases to exist. That's to say, your invested capital is still there, but it reverts to the pocket of your provider; it does **not** form part of your estate and your beneficiaries will therefore get none of it. (A joint life annuity will be passed on, but the overall rate is lower than with single life.)

So, be under no illusion that those who have been selling annuities, working for the provider, have quite possibly been focused not on giving you the most appropriate pension plan, but on securing the best deal for their employer – usually a single-life annuity.

"It's deeply dysfunctional for the consumer, but seems to be working very well for those who are selling annuities.

The mis-selling of annuities could be at least as big as the mis-selling of PPI."

Dr. Ros Altman, Pensions Expert, November 2013

And it's not just the single life annuities that may have been mis-sold. In November 2013, The Telegraph estimated that insurers made around £63m a year by directing unhealthy customers to an annuity designed for 'super-healthy' people. Research data from the Financial Conduct Authority, released in February 2014, showed that while 60 percent of people should qualify for an enhanced annuity because of poor health or an unhealthy lifestyle, just 7 percent of those who held pension savings at one of the ten firms that offer the enhancement had an annuity that took their medical condition into account.

Reporting from the same FCA data, in February 2014 thisismoney. co.uk said: 'around 1,000 retirees a day are being lured into payouts offered by their own insurer and are so confused that they fail to look elsewhere for the best deal.' And by taking the first option offered to them, some people are ending up on annuity deals that are around 20% below what they could get if they shopped around. The article went on to suggest the introduction of a 'pensions passport', where people would have to give information about their current pension provision, plus their health and lifestyle, in order that financial advisors and pension providers could give better, more tailored advice.

"Not only does [a passport] force the saver to engage with their savings, but it sends the message that this money is yours. It's up to you what you do with it. We've got to break the link between building up your pension savings, then taking them as an income. They are two different things, but are not treated as such — and that is where many problems lie."

Tom McPhail, head of pensions at Hargreaves Lansdown

In short, the industry seems to be admitting that people have not been getting the right pensions advice, acknowledging there is a widespread belief out there among savers that (a) annuities are the only option and (b) brokers are selling them an appropriate product. And that's just not true.

Quite apart from the risk of having been mis-sold your annuity, there is also the fact that the vast majority simply don't give a very good return.

"The annuity concept was designed for an era when life expectancy was much shorter than today. There is a serious question over whether people should be buying what is a low-risk, low-return product."

Otto Thorensen, Director General, The Association of British Insurers, February 2014

Now that we can expect to live to around 80 and most of us would like to retire as early as possible, you should probably plan for at least 25 years of living on your pension – and by that I mean your savings and various investments. And if you've invested in a traditional pension scheme, your money will be in a fund.

Fundamental problems with funds

Your (and your employer's / the state's) contributions are invested into funds, usually made up of stocks and shares in a broad range of companies, varying in terms of size, sector and geographical location.

The idea of these funds is that they comprise a balanced portfolio that carries minimal risk, due to its spread of interests, while still offering what is deemed a 'reasonable' return. The assumption is that that's what most people want: the safety of their capital virtually guaranteed, for a slightly better guaranteed return than they could get elsewhere. The problem is, 'reasonable' is likely to be inadequate – after all, it's almost always the case that the lower the risk, the lower the return. If you've only got to get by for ten years or so, the return offered by a standard annuity might suffice, especially if you've built up some other capital. But what about when you're looking at more than 20 years of living a decent lifestyle?

Then, these 'reasonable' returns are taxed and, of course, pension providers and brokers have to make money, so you pay fees for having your money invested and managed. That sounds fair enough, but the reality is you may be paying far more than you should.

In September 2013, the OFT revealed that around £30 billion of savers' money is still invested in 'old, high-charging workplace pension schemes' (those set up before 2001) and in February 2014, The Telegraph reported that fees charged by pension fund managers had risen by 'up to ten percent in two years'. Although the pensions minister has pledged to cap fees from April 2015, I can't help but think that the providers will simply find another way to recoup their subsequent profit shortfall.

And what about the people taking these fees and the companies they're investing your money into?

Periodically, over the past hundred years, institutions regarded as absolutely reliable because they were so big and wealthy have suffered massive drops in value, resulting in black days, crashes and crunches that have had a significant impact on both individuals and entire economies. The point is, companies can fail on an enormous scale, taking your money with them.

The failure of companies and institutions is usually down to human error – either gross incompetence or fraud – and these are people you will never meet. You're far removed from your investments, which are often made by brokers you don't know and possibly managed by other people you've never met, meaning you have very little control. And, because many of us struggle to understand pension products in any detail, we're almost forced to rely on the assumption that the people selling the products are offering us the best and most appropriate deal....and too many simply aren't at the moment.

"We have the opportunity to develop products and services that really meet people's needs - that are simpler, more flexible, and better value with transparent charges. And the opportunity to change the conversation on pensions so it's simple and more positive."

Ruston Smith, chairman, National Association of Pension Funds, December 2013

That's certainly the right sentiment, but are you prepared to wait until the Government and all the various financial institutions involved finally come up with new options that may only end up being marginally better than the current schemes?

The final kick in the teeth from workplace and other pension schemes is that if you want to cash them in early to invest the money into something else, known as 'pension liberation', the Government taxes the whole value of your pension pot at 55% and the pension company will take a large management or arrangement fee, which could be as much as a third of the total value. For example:

Value of pension pot at age 55:	£200,000
Less HMRC tax at 55%	£110,000
Less pension company fee of 30%	£60,000
Amount left for you to reinvest	£30,000

In other words, the financial penalties are so high that once you've built up a pension pot, you're essentially trapped in the scheme. Between them, pension providers and the Government have made sure you can't afford to change your mind or access any of **your** money until the originally agreed date – and then it's in small monthly amounts. Some changes to early release legislation have recently been made, but it's still not good enough to temp me to change my mind. This lack of flexibility and locking up of your savings is probably the single biggest reason I don't subscribe to a traditional pension scheme.

And lastly…

…a quick glance at the State Pension, such as it is. First things first: it's not very much at all. For the financial year 2013/14, the maximum amount a single person can draw is £110.15 a week. I don't know about you, but I certainly wouldn't want to have to try to live on that.

Then you have to think about the fact that there are fewer people paying in than drawing out and the gap between those two figures is getting wider every year. Even if there is still a 'state pension' by the time I retire, it's unlikely to bear much resemblance to what we have now. I'm working on the assumption that it will be such a small amount it's not really worth counting – and that's my recommendation to you: think of it as nothing more than a small added bonus that you may or may not get.

KEY NOTES

- Revisit and question your current pension provision

- If you haven't already, put together a personal financial statement

- Be aware: single-life annuities die with you – there is no capital to pass on to your family

- Your annuity may have been mis-sold, so question your provider

- Are you aware of all the fees, charges and taxes applied to your pension fund?

- Companies can fold and disappear overnight, taking all your money that's been invested in their stocks and shares with them

- You may as well forget the state pension!

ADDENDUM: Just as I was finishing this book, it was announced that savers – under certain conditions - will now be given 'unrestricted access' to their pension funds, with no draw down limits. This is excellent news for those who have an idea of what they would like to do with their capital instead of leaving it in their current scheme and a step in the right direction by the Government. However, I would suggest that pension providers are unlikely to have agreed to take a huge drop in profits, so I suspect they'll still be making money from their investors somewhere along the line… these things are rarely quite what they seem…

Chapter 3

Why property?

"Average [capital] gains of more than £7,000 in the [last] year highlights how property wealth can play a major role in improving the standard of living in retirement. On average, retired homeowners have gained nearly £600 a month, which compares very well with every other source of retirement income."

Dean Mirfin, Group Director, Key Retirement Solutions, February 2014

Property has long been considered a good investment, but why? "Because the value will go up over time" is the most common reasoning, but then people often stumble over being able to say much more, in the same way that they do when you ask why it's sensible to put money into a pension scheme!

What I'm going to explain in this chapter is why *I've* chosen to invest in property and to rely on it for the majority of my future financial security. Property investment success, in my opinion, comes down to understanding these key points, implementing them and incorporating them effectively within your investment strategy.

Leverage

I'm hesitant to choose a 'top' reason why property is such a good investment vehicle, but if I absolutely had to, then leverage would be it. There is not one other asset class that enables you to profit to the same extent from other people's money, while investing such a relatively low amount yourself, and at such a relatively low level of risk.

Banks and building societies lend against property at such a high Loan to Value rate because it's considered to have a fundamental 'bricks & mortar' value. The higher the LTV, the more confidence it demonstrates they have in the property market, because they will only lend what they can be sure they can recoup if you were to default and they had to sell. As a result of their confidence, you can leverage their money to make a better return on your own capital than you could in almost any other situation, because when the market rises you get to keep *all* the profit (less, tax, of course!), not just the profit on your share of the capital investment.

Let's say there was a rise of 15% across all markets and you had invested £100k in stocks, you would benefit from growth of £15k, i.e. your capital would have increased by 15%. But if you had split that £100k investment capital into 25% deposits on four properties, each worth £100k, that would be a total of £60k growth, representing a 60% increase on your original investment. Even taking into account that realising that profit would involve paying taxes and fees, you would still be many times better off having invested in property than if you had put your money in stocks.

In short, the power of leverage means your money goes further and enables you to invest in assets with a value that's several times that of your actual capital – which brings me on to the next major benefit of property: the ability to refinance.

Refinancing

The willingness of lenders to loan you such a high proportion of a property's value means that when it increases in value, you should be able to remortgage and extract some of your invested capital. There needs to be sufficient equity for the LTV of the mortgage product and the rental income must 'stack up' (see Chapter 4), but as long as you and the property can satisfy the lender's criteria, this is a great facility.

While there is an administrative cost associated with refinancing – broker fees, lender fees and survey fees – and there are likely to be tax implications down the line, the cost is nothing like the prohibitively heavy penalties you suffer if you want to release lump sums from your pension. I wouldn't recommend doing it on a regular basis, but certainly it's worth looking at the possibility every three to five years.

If you've bought 'well' and treat the property as a medium to long-term investment (and assuming the market continues to rise over time), you should find that at some point you are able to release all the capital you originally put in, leaving you with an appreciating and possibly income-producing asset that has none of your own money tied up in it. You can then take the lump sum you release and either reinvest or spend it.

Leverage and refinancing together certainly make a strong argument for property offering the best potential return on your capital, but add in the income opportunity and that's when property really becomes an exciting investment proposition.

Income returns

With all other asset classes, you mainly profit from growth on the capital. Although there may be interest payments on other types of investment, I haven't found any that offer the same income potential as property, where your tenants' rent covers the mortgage and other costs associated with the property and there is enough left over, after tax, for you to take a good profit.

The caveat to that is: you get out what you put in. That's to say, in order to get the best income returns, you'll need to invest time and effort and put an effective business management system in place, which I'll go on to describe in Chapter 4. You incur far more costs in running a high income-generating portfolio of buy to let properties – and I'm talking about multi-lets - but the profit is much greater than if you take a hands-off approach.

There's a lot to consider in making the decision about how involved to be in your investments (see Chapter 8), but if you're able and prepared to build a property business, it can give you on-going monthly income at a level that will cover all your own bills, and many of your other outgoings. Put that together with the possibility of refinancing and I'd say that within five to seven years you could be looking at a situation where you have a portfolio of appreciating assets giving you a more or less passive income, with most, if not all of your original capital released. Now that's a good investment.

'The average £30,000 pot provides an annuity income of around £1,500 a year. In reality, that's a menial top-up to the state pension and it takes 20 years before you get back what you put in.'

The Telegraph, 4ᵗʰ February 2014

In contrast, if you could use that £30,000 to put down a 15% deposit on an investment property, assuming you 'bought well', it's quite possible you would be able to:

- generate at least £125 monthly income, equivalent to the annuity payment
- secure an asset that would appreciate in value, in addition to providing income

- retain the invested £30,000 capital and still be able to access it via sale, equity release or refinancing
- have the option of passing on the whole amount to your family

Variety and flexibility of opportunities

One of the big downsides of saving in a traditional pension scheme is the inflexibility of it. You're expected to decide, at a relatively early stage in your working life, on a plan that will stay more or less the same until you retire. If you decide – and it may be years down the line - that you want to change to a different plan or gain access to *your* money, the financial penalties can be huge. You are also in the hands of other people and have very little control over where your money is ultimately invested.

Property, on the other hand, is a brilliantly flexible asset class. Not only do you decide on the type of property you buy, but also what you do with it and when. That means **you** have control over how you make your returns and when and how you take them.

While you can't control the market as a whole or mortgage rates, you *can* choose:
- residential or commercial property
- the type of property
- the location of the property
- your mortgage product

- how much you invest in improving/refurbishing
- what type of tenants you accept
- the rent you charge (to a certain extent)

All that means you have a very high degree of control over income and expenditure, and therefore profitability. Your income is not at the beck & call of the stock market, as are annuity payments.

Although there are planning issues to consider, which will limit your options, a property is essentially square footage, which you could look at as nothing more than a potentially profitable box. That means you can, to a certain extent, change your mind about how you make money from it and move with the demand from the market.

For example, there is currently a very high demand from young working adults for rooms in shared houses, with an all-inclusive rent package. As a result, some landlords are turning what were previously let as family homes, into multi-let accommodation, satisfying local demand and increasing their income in the process. There is also the opportunity in many areas to convert commercial premises into residential accommodation, as well as deals to be done to raze an existing property to the ground and either build a new property yourself, or simply gain planning and sell on.

I thought carefully about the way I wanted to structure my own portfolio and my property knowledge has meant I've been able to make better decisions in my other businesses, to give me greater financial security.

In addition to the single and multi-let rental properties I own, I also took the decision to buy premises for my childcare business, rather than renting. As a result, my business pays me rent and I have chosen a property that will also let well as a House in Multiple Occupation, should I move the business in the future.

Having this level of control and such a variety of options is yet another key reason why so many people use property as a wealth creation tool. Your future financial requirements change as your life circumstances change, and property allows you to change your mind accordingly.

A tangible, appreciating asset

The last point brings me back to where I started – with the fact that property has always gone up in value over the long term. People will always need a roof over their heads and there's a finite amount of land available for development. Of course, not every property in every area will increase in value at the same rate – and some will undoubtedly fall, for a variety of reasons – so calling property an appreciating asset comes with a caveat: it's all in the buying.

Properties appreciate in value because they're in demand and there is a skill in identifying a property that you can be confident will remain in demand into the future. Even if your focus is on buying properties that will primarily give you income, you need to be as sure as possible that they will also increase in value so that your investment at least keeps pace with the market. That requires good local area knowledge and contacts, market research and an understanding of some fundamental economic principles….all of which you should be perfectly capable of acquiring yourself.

And that ties in with my previous points about having control - you can decide exactly where you put your money; you're not relying on anyone else for your investment. Now, you may see that as a good or a bad thing, and you're quite right! Because if you really don't know what you're doing and don't have the time or the inclination to carry out the necessary research, property may not be the best investment vehicle for you. You don't get something for nothing (I'll discuss working with companies that offer 'passive' investments later in the book) and, like any investment, the best property investments are made through expertise. And the more expertise you can gain yourself, the more control you will have.

And, finally, I *like* that property is tangible. You can see it, touch it, appreciate its aesthetic qualities and anything that is tangible retains an intrinsic value, unlike stocks, which can lose all their value frighteningly quickly. The fact that I can drive around the area and look at my investments, rather than simply figures on a spreadsheet, gives me confidence that I'm building a solid financial future.

"Real estate cannot be lost or stolen, nor can it be carried away. Purchased with common sense and managed with reasonable care, it is about the safest investment in the world."

Franklin D. Roosevelt

Demand for accommodation from the Private Rented Sector (PRS)

The arguments I'm making here for property are dependent on one major factor: the presence of demand. You can only refinance, benefit from capital appreciation and secure income from property if you have tenants and buyers demanding a supply of the particular kind of accommodation you have. As such, each different kind of property investment strategy will require research into the specific demand from the 'end customer', which I'll talk about as we look at each one. But the overall picture for landlords is very good: the demand for rental accommodation within the private rented sector has never been higher and that looks likely to continue for the foreseeable future.

'More people now rent privately than from councils or housing associations'

The Independent, 26th February 2014

'Fuelled by rising house prices, demographic change and a tight mortgage market, demand for renting has doubled the size of the PRS over the last decade.'

The Guardian, 26th February 2014

Figure 1: Trends in tenure, 1980 to 2012-13

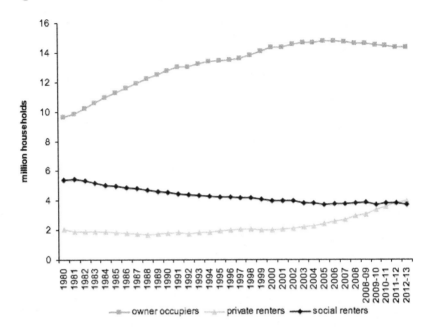

Source: DCLG English Housing Survey Report 2012-13

The chart above shows that in 2012 the number of households (and a 'household' can be a family or an individual) renting from private landlords rose above that of those renting social housing for the first time since records began. You can also clearly see that the PRS has been growing steadily over the past thirty years, while levels of available social housing have fallen and the number of owner-occupiers has dropped slightly since the highs of the mid-2000s. But to be able to assess whether this demand will continue into the future – and at least for the lifetime of your proposed investment – we need to understand the key reasons behind the trends.

Shortage of new housing

The headline fact here is that we have been consistently failing to meet new house-building targets for too long. Taking an average of the figures calculated by various local and national housing and planning organisations, we need to build around 250,000 new homes each year to keep up with the growth in households and ensure prices remain affordable.

DCLG Household Interim Projections 2013 stated that the number of households in England is projected to grow by 221,000 a year from 2011 to 2021. In 2011, total new housing completions stood at 114,000 (only 25% of which was by local authorities and housing associations); from 2011 to 2012 NHBC reported a decrease in new home registrations, and the latest figures show a further drop:

'Annual housing completions in England totalled 109,370 in the 12 months to December 2013, 5% lower compared to the previous 12 months.'

DCLG House Building report, published February 2014

Lack of affordability

The fundamental shortage in the supply of new housing has been the key contributing factor to the rise in house prices, which has had the knock-on effect of taking the cost of owning their own home beyond the reach of many people. The average house price in the UK, as I write, is around £170,000* and, while 95% mortgages are available, in order to benefit from what is considered a more 'reasonable' interest rate, you really need to be putting down a deposit of 15%, or more. That means, at the highest rate of borrowing, people need to have an average of £8,500 in deposit funds; 85% borrowing on the average house price requires £25,500. On top of that, there's Stamp Duty Land Tax, removals, legal and mortgage fees and other variable moving costs.

In 1983, the average deposit was around 12% of average national income. Today, that figure stands at 82%**.

And after the introduction of the 'Help to Buy' schemes and various incentives designed to get the property market moving – and particularly aimed at getting first time buyers on the ladder – it has recently been announced in the media that mortgage lenders have tightened their criteria, to ensure borrowers will be able to afford their repayments on-going - the assumption being that interest rates can only increase. Financial commitments, such as gym memberships and childcare are likely to be taken into consideration, as well as other 'lifestyle' outgoings, including what's regularly being spent on travel and entertainment.

In short, it seems that after the last credit crunch crisis, the Financial Conduct Authority (FCA) is keener than ever to ensure banks lend responsibly. And while that's certainly a fundamentally good position, it means there's going to have to be some more creative thinking about how to address the affordability problem.

(* Source: Land Registry, February 2014; ** Source: The Telegraph, February 2014.)

Shortage of social housing

Some of the increase in demand has come from those who can't afford to buy their own home – and there is a particularly high demand from those in their twenties and thirties, as a result of a big jump in the birth rate in the 1980s - but there is also a significant demand from those who are fundamentally unable or unwilling to buy a home.

The Thatcher government's legislation allowing council tenants the 'Right to Buy' their homes is often cited as a reason behind the current lack of supply of social housing but, while it's a factor, I don't think it's the biggest cause. Around 1.5 million homes have been bought under the scheme, reducing the stock that would have become available as existing tenants died or their circumstances changed and they were able to move on. But from 1980, when Right to Buy was introduced, to 2012, the population of Great Britain increased by around 7 million, and it's this population increase that has had far more of an impact, in my opinion.

While the building of social housing has fallen way short of targets, the number of households needing it has grown faster than anticipated. Between 1991 and 2012, 3.4m people migrated to the UK – that's more than half the total population growth figure for that period – and many of those have needed to be housed by local authorities, on top of the demand from UK nationals. According to Shelter, 'there are more than 1.8m households waiting for a social home – an increase of 81% since 1997'.

And so, because of this lack of supply of social housing, there is a huge demand for affordable accommodation from the private rented sector. While the rent that can be charged to social tenants may not be quite as high as could be asked of private tenants, many local authorities will make payments direct to the landlord and take out long-term agreements, so the issues of rent defaults and void periods are virtually eliminated. As such, many private landlords are accepting social tenants and finding it a solid proposition – and something they can rely on into the future.

Transient working population

And finally, there is the way our working lives have changed. Many more people than ever before move around the UK for work and/ or are on short-term contracts with no certainty over what the next job or contract will be. And so there is an on-going demand for short to medium-term rental accommodation from working adults who need the flexibility to be able to move on quickly and easily, sometimes at short notice, as their work changes.

These people are often perfectly able to pay rent at the top end of the market and are quite prepared to do so for good-quality accommodation. Those who can't afford to put down large deposits and don't want to have to worry about variable costs and rising bills are often very keen to take an all-inclusive rent package within a shared house. In short, there is demand from the transient working population for a variety of rental property and it's a demand that seems likely to keep growing.

KEY NOTES

- Property is the only asset class against which you can borrow at such a high level and benefit from **all** the capital growth (less tax, of course!)

- You should be able to refinance at some point and could end up with an income-producing asset that's growing in value, with none of your own money invested in it

- Property is an incredibly flexible, tangible investment vehicle

- You have a high degree of control over your asset and its associated income and expenditure – and, therefore, profit

- There is a very real shortage of housing stock and an increasing demand

- On-going lack of affordability of home ownership means a stable on-going rental demand

Part Two will go on to explore the different kinds of property investment you can make and the various types of return each can give you and will, I hope, enable you to make some basic decisions about what might be the right route for you to take yourself. For me, property undoubtedly offers the most reliable, tangible, flexible, profitable form of investment I've been able to find. It suits my lifestyle, work ethic, skills, risk profile, personality, tax situation, pension provision and inheritance plans for my children – and these are all things you need to consider carefully as you read on.

PART TWO:

YOUR PROPERTY INVESTMENT OPTIONS

Chapter 4

Investing for income

A lot of people think about property primarily in terms of capital appreciation and consider their current property assets as something to be held and then 'cashed in' through selling or releasing equity. Lump sum returns of that kind are great and should certainly form part of your investment plan but, in the same way that businesses survive on cash flow, so do we!

The main concern most of us have for our retirement is: when we stop earning a monthly salary, where is our regular income going to come from? Well, depending on what you buy and how you let it, property can deliver anything from a pension top-up to a monthly income that exceeds what you earned as an employee. That's why increasing numbers of people are now using property as their primary investment vehicle.

The income strategy depends on a demand for a certain type of rental accommodation, because the best returns are usually achieved through offering shared housing, where tenants rent individual bedrooms and share the other living facilities. By renting out a property in this way, you can expect to bring in two to three times the rent you would receive from letting it as a single unit. With all buy to let you need to carefully analyse the demand - what it's like now and what it's likely to be in the future – but if you're looking to generate income, your research is especially important. If you make a mistake with this, you could find your standard of living compromised. That being said, there's no reason why you should get it wrong if you do your homework!

Be under no illusion; property investment – particularly when you're talking about an income-generating portfolio - is a business and needs to be treated as such. I invest in several different businesses – some I'm directly involved with; some I have simply financed – but property is where I spend most of my time and effort. I've got a fantastic team that help me run the business, so I don't need to worry about the day-to-day letting and management of my buy to let properties, but managing that team and taking care of all the administrative and financial implications of owning and trading in assets requires fundamental business skills. Of course, there are options for taking a more 'hands off' approach to investing - and I'll cover those in more detail later on – but if you're looking for income from property, that's a business in itself.

Houses in Multiple Occupation (HMOs)

Most shared houses are HMOs. The Government considers a property an HMO if there are three or more tenants living there, forming more than one household (i.e. they're unrelated) and they're sharing toilet, bathroom or kitchen facilities. If a building has three or more storeys and is occupied by five or more people, forming two or more households, the HMO must be licensed. Those are the umbrella definitions but, practically, it's a bit more complicated, because precise criteria for licensing can vary wildly from council to council, as can the criteria for needing planning permission for change of use class. What you do and don't need to do in terms of health and safety can also be largely dependent on the attitude of the personnel in your own local council and fire safety departments and there is currently no nationwide system for councils to make checks on HMOs.

And all of that regulation and inconsistency is a big reason why many investors steer clear of HMOs, but I think they're making a mistake. Yes, there's a lot to comply with and keep track of, the management is more time consuming and your costs are higher, but the profit levels really do make it worthwhile, in my opinion.

The best returns, as far as HMOs are concerned, tend to come from renting to working adults. You provide them with a room of their own, at a rate that includes all their utility bills and council tax, and then they share the kitchen, bathroom facilities and possibly another communal area, such as a sitting room. And there's an increasing demand for this kind of accommodation, which gives tenants the security of fixed outgoings and the convenience of more flexible terms, with most HMO landlords only asking for a month's notice if a someone wants to leave. It also provides a sociable environment, living with like-minded people.

Social housing tenants

For a long time, professional landlords shied away from renting to tenants who are dependent on housing benefit, but these days it can be a good way of ensuring a consistent level of 'secure' rental income. Many local authorities will pay rent direct to landlords and in some areas this can be at a good level, compared with what can be achieved by renting to tenants paying privately. Social housing tenants also tend to stay for longer, meaning less re-letting administration.

To find out more about providing high revenue-generating, shared accommodation for working adults, read my first book, **'HMO Property Success: The proven strategy for financial freedom from multi-let property investing'** – available in paperback and Kindle from amazon.co.uk and on iBook, via iTunes.

The main potential downsides are that if the tenants come off benefits, they may not be used to planning their own finances and may struggle to pay their rent in full and on time. They may also be in the property for more of the day than those who are in work, meaning utility bills could be higher and there might be more wear and tear on fixtures, fittings and furnishings.

I meet a lot of landlords who let at least one of the HMOs in their portfolio to tenants on housing benefit, because they see it as helping the local community, and that's a pretty decent attitude to have. While some people are quick to point out the risks, there are always risks in this business – some of the worst 'bad tenants' are those who seem the most respectable at first. So just do your due diligence, make sure that you're very clear about what's expected and trust your gut instinct when deciding whether to accept someone who's applying to live in your property.

What I would say is, don't mix tenant types. Shared houses work best when people have similar lifestyles and it's much easier to manage tenants when everyone's more or less on the same page.

Student letting

The most common perception of HMOs is that they're student houses and in college and university towns and cities student letting can be very profitable.

People often take the attitude that students treat properties badly, party all the time and can't afford to pay very much rent, but, in reality, the reverse is true. You can usually insist on parents acting as guarantors, which means you have security for payment of rent and are highly unlikely to get defaults. Also, they're usually under one AST, so are jointly and severally liable for the rent, which gives you an added layer of security, as students will generally ensure everyone pays! They also tend to treat the property quite well because they – and their parents! - want their deposits returned.

Another reason landlords often give for not wanting student lets is the risk of voids between academic years, but many students – particularly those in their final year – prefer to hold and/or stay in their accommodation over the summer, for both social and study reasons, particularly if they have part-time jobs. If you do have a month or two between full-time student lets, you may be able to offer short-term lets to foreign students on summer language courses. A short gap also gives you the opportunity to carry out repairs and refresh the property so that you can re-let quickly at the best price and have your pick of prospective tenants! Students almost always want to secure accommodation well in advance of the new academic year, so if you can assure them they'll be moving into an updated home, you should attract a lot of enquiries.

And don't be tempted to think that you can get away with spending far less on refurbishment and maintenance, simply because 'they're only students'. Students these days have an increasingly large choice of where to live and the condition of the property is a big factor for them, so give them a nice home. A good yardstick is, would you be happy for a child of yours to live there?

The main risk in student letting is that areas can end up with a big over-supply of property if colleges and universities decide to build their own halls/accommodation. You may be able to switch your HMO tenant type to working adults but it's likely that the area won't be right if there's a heavy student population. In short, before you buy a student property, check the future plans for the university/college and the area very carefully.

NUS research into students' experiences of renting

In March 2014, the National Union of Students published the results of the first ever piece of research commissioned into student letting. It looked at their needs and made recommendations for how the experience could be improved for them, at every stage of the rental process. Some headline facts and figures:

- 44% of students rent from the PRS
- Choice between PRS or other accommodation is based on 1) location, 2) cost, 3) ease of rental
- They choose a specific PRS property based on 1) price, 2) location and 3) condition
- Three quarters of students have had to complain about a property's condition – usually about damp and cold
- Around 20% felt pressurised into either signing a contract or paying a holding fee before they'd seen the contract
- Around half didn't know whether they'd had a copy of the EPC
- More than a third went into debt to secure a property
- Around half had to pay fees they didn't know about in advance
- Only just over half were sure their deposit had been protected.

Most of the students surveyed were happy overall with their PRS accommodation, but the vast majority thought there should be a minimum condition standard, a ban on fees and more services to ensure landlords fulfilled their responsibilities.

Systemisation

I've already said that letting for income is a business and the key to building a profitable portfolio is systemisation. There is a lot of work to do and, while you can probably handle it yourself for the first few properties, it can quickly become a full-time job if you're not careful. The idea of investing in high-income generating properties is that it gives you a greater level of financial freedom, not that you kill yourself achieving it!

You need to build a team who can keep the business ticking over nicely without you having to be there every day. The success and effectiveness of that team will depend on there being a system that they understand and follow, for every stage of the process, from sourcing to marketing to on-going management, and everything in between.

You can either spend some time with people like me, who have been there already, refined systems through trial and error and have an effective system in place that you can replicate, or you can go through that process yourself. It's certainly possible – I did it! – but you'll get there a lot more quickly if you take advantage of someone else's experience.

Expanding your business

Once you have the right business model and the right people in place, your main role should simply be managing those people and the profits, whether that means choosing where and how to reinvest them or spending them. And having a good system means it's easy for you to scale up your business and add more properties to the portfolio.

In addition to buying more properties of your own, a simple way to generate more income is to take on the full management of other landlords' properties. You're already got the system – you're just adding more accommodation to it. A greater variety of accommodation will attract more tenants, which will raise your profile as a high-quality landlord. And that should contribute very well to helping you maximize profitability.

Yes, a multi-let property portfolio will never be quite as 'hands off' as most other investments, regardless of how good your systems are, but the income and capital appreciation should more than make up for that. I'll move on to more 'passive' investment options in chapters 6 and 7; next, let's take a look at lump-sum returns in the short to medium term.

KEY NOTES

- You must appreciate that investing for income is a business in itself

- HMOs are a very specific type of rental property and subject to specific governance, which has both national and local regulations

- Research really is key when you're relying on property to generate a certain level of on-going income. Take the time to properly analyse the local market and the demand for shared housing.

- Look to other successful portfolio landlords who have established business systems in place and replicate those systems

- For much more information about HMOs, read my first book, **'HMO Property Success'**, available on Amazon and iTunes

Chapter 5

Investing for lump-sum returns in the short to medium term

The perfect investment for most people would be one that gives a healthy income and also grows well in value. Unfortunately, it's *very* rare to find something that can deliver both at a good level, so how those two things are balanced will depend on your personal needs and investment goals.

Generally speaking (and I'm taking London out of the equation), if a property is in an area where multi-let rental prices are high, it's unlikely to be the kind of highly desirable area where capital values rise quickly. Similarly, when the property market is on the rise, it's owner-occupied homes that are in demand and those don't tend to be the kind of properties that deliver brilliant income.

So you need to be clear on your main focus every time you buy a property: is it primarily for income or for a lump sum return? And if it's the latter, **when** do you want your return and **how much** do you need? I'll cover investment planning in more detail in Chapter 10; in this chapter, we're looking at how property can deliver you a lump sum return in the short to medium term – by which, I mean 1-5 years.

As a general rule, you should view property as a medium to long-term investment because it takes time for average property values to rise and most people have chosen to invest in property because they're confident of that increase in equity over time. However, it's useful to work some options for shorter-term returns into your investment portfolio, if for no other reason than to spread your risk. Plans are great, but they can change and you don't want to find yourself 'trapped' and unable to access some capital if you need to.

Buying to improve and sell

This strategy was incredibly popular in the 1990s and early 2000s. Prices were increasing at such a rate that anyone with some capital to invest could buy a property that needed work - from simple cosmetic improvements to complete renovation projects – and sell as soon as the work was done for a significant profit.

Programmes like 'Changing Rooms', 'Property Ladder' and 'Trading Up' on television fuelled people's imaginations and sold the dream that anyone could make money by improving a property, which a great many did. However, exactly how much of the uplift in value was due to the extent and quality of the work and how much was due to the naturally rising market was never explored, and that's why you need to be very careful with this strategy. You don't want to end up spending more time and money than it's worth, once you've factored in inflation.

So what should I buy?

You usually make the most money by buying a property that most people don't want and selling it on once you've turned it into something that's in huge demand. What you need to assess is whether you have the capital and the capability to turn one into the other – and what return you're likely to get for your trouble.

Nowadays, you really have to try to find projects that need as close to a complete renovation as possible; you can't just do cosmetic work. DIY stores and suppliers have come a long way in the last 20 years in terms of the range of products, tools and services that they offer, and most people are prepared to tackle re-plastering, new kitchens and bathrooms and redecoration themselves – it's not something they'll pay over the odds for. So look for a property that needs more serious building work, new electrics and plumbing – the kind of work that requires specialist contractors and a good amount of capital spending on it.

Often, people look at auctions for this kind of property, although more and more people are looking for something they can make into their own perfect home, so bear in mind you could find yourself bidding against people with an emotional investment, who are therefore probably prepared to pay over the odds. So make sure you do your research, work out the maximum price at which the property would still stack up as a good investment and don't get lured into a bidding war!

A few other points to bear in mind if you decide to buy at auction:

- When the hammer falls you are liable for a 10% deposit in cash, so you need to have it instantly available
- The sale is immediate and there's no come-back if you find the property is in worse condition than you thought, so make sure you carry out a survey and any other research ahead of the auction
- The 90% balance is usually due within 28 days of the sale, therefore you need to have a mortgage agreement lined up and be confident that your broker or FA can push the transaction thorough in time, otherwise there will be penalties.

A great many complete renovation projects were bought and completed in the last 10-15 years and there simply isn't the amount of stock needing 'serious attention' that there used to be, so there's likely to be competition from other investors for this kind of property. Builders in particular, who can get materials at cost and labour for free, might get the property you want because they can afford to pay slightly more for it and still make more profit than you would! So it might take some time to find the right project that stacks up financially and that's why, if you're looking at a buy/improve/sell strategy, it's a good idea to have something else in the works as well or you can get frustrated at not having an investment underway.

Don't put all your eggs in one basket...

Before I move on, I just want to stress that it really isn't a good idea, especially in the current economic climate, to rely solely on this property investment strategy. Because of the costs you're incurring over a relatively short period of time, you really should only buy and sell quickly in a rising market, where natural price inflation helps insulate you against anything going wrong with your plans. Having other income-producing properties up and running before you embark on buying to improve and sell is certainly the smart move, as far as I'm concerned.

Buying below true value, holding, then refinancing or selling

You've probably heard about 'BMV' deals, usually linked to 'dodgy passive investment companies'. Six or seven years ago it was possible to buy a property at one price, secure a valuation at a significantly higher price and refinance on the day you completed with a mortgage based on the higher valuation, essentially buying 'no money down'. Plenty of people took advantage of this loophole and so-called 'professional' individuals and investment companies sourced and facilitated deals for investors and themselves, building portfolios that had none – or very little – of their own capital invested in them.

The days of 'no money down' are over and that financing option, along with a number of other 'creative' alternatives that achieved much the same result, is no longer available.

However, if you're in a strong buying position – with nothing to sell, a good team of legal and financial advisors behind you and money to invest – and a vendor *has* to sell, for personal or financial reasons, you can still negotiate a good deal for yourself. You'll get the best discounts when the market is at its peak, with an excess of supply over demand, but I've found that there are always deals to be done if you have the right approach.

When I say 'true value', I don't mean the asking price, I mean the value a surveyor would put on it. When you've researched properties in an area and after you've bought one or two, you develop a gut instinct for what they're worth, but what's important here is the value a surveyor would pass on to a mortgage company.

I cover how to assess a property's value, negotiation techniques and putting forward offers in my first book, 'HMO PROPERTY SUCCESS', so visit nickfox.co.uk to find out how to get hold of it, in paperback, digital and audio versions.

So this strategy is, essentially, buying something that has equity built in from the outset and either refinancing to release that equity or selling to realise the profit. Most lenders will make you wait at least 6 months before you can refinance and, even then, there may be redemption penalties to pay, so make sure you check those implications with your financial advisor or mortgage broker when you're assessing the deal.

Typically, the best discounted deals are achieved on modest properties that are suitable for a single let, rather than larger property that you could let as an HMO. That means you're not likely to achieve much, if any income while you're waiting to release your money. However, you do need to do your research to ensure you'll be able to let it at a rate that at least covers your mortgage repayment and any other on-going costs. That means you should be able to afford to hold the property until any mortgage redemption penalty period has expired and maximise your return.

The kind of properties that you can buy at a discount also tend not to be in the best state of décor and/or repair, so while you're waiting to refinance or sell, you may be able to force some extra appreciation by making a few improvements. It's a good idea to speak to a local estate agent before you start, to find out exactly how much work it's worth doing; as with the 'improve & sell' strategy, you don't want to spend more than makes financial sense.

Self build and development

A lot of people dream of building their own home, but I'm not talking about the kind of thing you see on 'Grand Designs', where budgets get blown on making something fabulous and individual. The kind of new property that will make you good money is simple housing stock.

This country's Government has failed to even come close to its targets for new housing for several years now and the population is continuing to increase (see **Chapter 3: Shortage of new housing**). So there's no doubt the private sector needs to help out now, more than ever, in the supply of housing.

If you've got a decent amount of capital to invest in buying some land to develop, you'll get the biggest uplift in value by buying a brownfield site for which you then get planning. Planning is the main issue when you're acquiring land for development and, as with most investments, you win biggest when you take the biggest risks. I haven't yet bought any land on that basis, but that's not to say I wouldn't consider it in the future. You would need to know the area well and develop a good relationship with the local town and country planners to make sure it was as certain as possible permission to develop would be granted – and granted for the kind of housing you wanted to build. The last thing you want to end up with is a piece of land on which planning has been refused.

You should also look at the potential that could be unlocked in the land attached to any properties you either already own or are considering buying. If you have a property that's already giving a good return, you have little to lose in applying for planning. That will cost a few thousand pounds but if you get as good an idea as possible from the local planning department before you apply, then it could be money very well spent.

I have two gardens that I split from buy to let properties I own. With planning, a garden that hadn't really held much material value suddenly represented a extra £120k in equity! I haven't moved forward on this project yet; my current thinking is to sell to a builder and simply realise and reinvest the money, but I may partner with another investor or developer, or simply complete the build myself.

That's the beauty of investing in land – it gives you so many options and a variety of ways of making money. You can simply sell to a developer for a relatively quick and easy return; build yourself and sell the property on as soon as it's completed; partner with a developer or other investor to complete a build and then sell, possibly retaining the freehold; you may even decide to build high income-generating property, such as flats or HMOs, refinance the buildings on completion and keep hold of them for income. Then you're a real property tycoon!

"Buy land, they're not making it any more."

Mark Twain

Remember the cost implications

Before you get excited about the amount of money you could make on your investment over a relatively short period of time, remember to factor in all the costs. They're likely to include:

- Stamp Duty Land Tax on purchase
- Survey fees on purchase and possibly on renovation
- Planning & architects fees, possibly other building consultancy costs
- Legal fees on purchase and sale
- Estate agent fees
- Capital gains tax on disposal of the asset
- Possible penalty fees on early repayment of mortgage

…not to mention the costs of the actual renovation or construction.

It really is essential that you sit down right at the start with a financial advisor who is used to dealing with property investments or, even better, a wealth manager, so that you can plan the best investment route to take.

RICS' report says house prices will rise everywhere over the next five years, from 2 per cent a year in the North to 9.3 per cent a year in London.

Savills sees house prices rising by 25 per cent over five years across Britain, but adds that some areas will outstrip that.
thisismoney.co.uk, April 2014

KEY NOTES

- The short-term return strategy is a relatively risky one

- It tends to be capital intensive, so you will need some money behind you

- I would only recommend this strategy when you can be sure the market is rising at a good rate

- There is usually a lot of competition from other investors for the kind of property that will give shorter-term returns, so make sure you're in the best possible position to negotiate a purchase and keep persevering!

- Check out all the tax and mortgage cost implications with your financial advisor

- If you're looking to develop land, spend some time doing specific research and building a relationship with the local town and country planner(s)

- You might consider partnering with a local developer who already has the contacts to proceed efficiently with a build

Chapter 6

Investing for returns in the longer term

This really is the easiest property investment 'strategy'. If you're looking for long-term returns, property is a very low risk investment vehicle because virtually all property will give a decent capital growth return over a period of fifteen or more years. You'd have to be extremely unlucky not to make money from property simply by buying and holding it.

As I've said before, that's a key reason why property makes such an excellent investment. You can build a portfolio on the basis of an income strategy and make money month-on-month from buy to let, knowing that you'll also benefit from natural capital appreciation over the long term. The capital increase may not be as great with a multi-let property as it is with a more 'traditional' home, but that's why you should build a varied portfolio; so you can get different returns in different ways at different times.

Single-let units

This kind of property investment can be anything from a studio apartment to a large family home. The difference between letting a property to one individual, couple or family and letting something as an HMO is the monthly rental income. There are exceptions to the rule - mainly when you're talking about capital cities, where corporate let apartments and exclusive high-earner-style homes attract a premium – but, in the main, people invest in single lets as more of a pension pot. The rent might produce a little income, but it's the capital appreciation over the long term that investors are relying on.

It's virtually impossible to guarantee what kind of property is going to appreciate by the greatest percentage over the long term, but you can give yourself the best possible chance by following some fundamental principles. Properties that are short on supply and highly in demand from people who can afford to buy are the ones that will realise the highest gains, so it's a case of how to predict that future demand.

Assessing future demand

In the absence of a crystal ball, this means doing some solid research. The good news is that these days there are some very good information portals online. Take a look at your local council's development plans on their website, which will show all new job creation and infrastructure projects that the local authority is working on. Several estate agents and property consultants are also doing excellent research themselves, much of which is freely available to you. Savills, in particular, have a first-class department dedicated to analysing markets and producing reports, so it's well worth going into the nearest branch and speaking to them.

Look at where affordability is reasonable, in the middle range of the market, as these are the areas where most of the working population tends to settle and where they're likely to remain for the foreseeable future. Schools, hospitals and shopping centres don't tend to move, so properties with easy access to all three will probably be a very safe bet. Houses within the catchment of schools that have had a good reputation for a number of years are particularly desirable, tending to increase in value well and sell quickly.

I'd also recommend going for a property with a minimum of two bedrooms. Affordability for first time buyers has been an issue for around a decade now, whereas families and friends are more likely to be able to afford to buy together. And as people live longer and the availability and cost of care becomes more and more of an issue, we're seeing a trend towards elderly relatives moving back in with their children, so homes with three or more bedrooms and/or the potential for an annexe will be what middle-aged buyers will increasingly look for.

The other thing to bear in mind is that you may want or need to access the equity sooner than you planned to, so buying something that has a unique or at least rare quality will help give you the 'edge' if you need to sell quickly. They're not building Victorian or Edwardian properties any more, so going for a nice character property is a fairly safe bet. If you're going for a more modern home, perhaps something in a block or on a development, try to get one with a corner plot, extra parking or at the end of a cul de sac – just something that makes it a little more desirable than the neighbouring properties.

Those are some generally good principles but the fact is, each area has its own market and the property professionals working in that market are best placed to inform and advise you, so the most sensible thing for you to do is start building relationships with them.

Making sure you cover yourself in the meantime

Going hand in hand with your research into future demand in the sales market must be research into the likely rental demand from now until you're planning to dispose of the property. While your main focus for this investment is its capital gain, you must make sure the rental returns at least cover the costs of holding and maintaining the property, as well as keeping up with inflation. If you have to start subsidising the investment every month and/or the rent you can charge starts to be worth less and less to you in real terms, that's not a good investment.

Again, speaking to local letting agents should pretty much tell you all you need to know about the market, and do make sure you ask the simple question: 'What do you always need more of?'. In every area there will be a type of property that letting agents always wish they had more of on their books, so see whether that type of stock matches up with the type that looks like a good long-term sales prospect and you should have an ideal investment.

Beware the 'sourcers'

It may sound like a lot of work for you to research the investment yourself and there are plenty of companies and individuals who would be more than happy to put together deals for you. I'd steer clear. It really doesn't take much more time and effort to find properties yourself than it would take to check out the pedigree of these companies and deals. If this is their business, they're making a good profit from some stage of the deal – profit that you could be keeping for yourself.

I always recommend buying reasonably close to where you live, so that you can really get to know the market and build relationships, and you'll find that if you do that properly for your first investment, it'll be much, much easier when you come to make a second. Sourcers tend to either charge you a flat fee up front or take a percentage of the value of the deal, which means they have their money and it doesn't make any difference to them whether the investment works out or not. There are a few companies that retain an interest in the property and offer to manage the whole purchase process and management for you but, in my opinion, these are usually incredibly bad value for money. I've yet to see one I'd recommend to anyone.

Commercial property

A buzz about commercial investing began a few years ago in the investment community, I think mainly because people were looking to diversify their portfolios and fancied something different to residential buy to let.

Investing in commercial property is certainly a good way to diversify your portfolio, as it's a different kind of property market. The value is based on not just the bricks and mortar value of the property itself but also on the quality of the tenant and length of the lease. That means there is the potential to buy something with a short lease remaining and modest rent, make some improvements to the property to attract a better, different kind of tenant and add significant value to your investment.

Commercial lets are often said to be more stable than residential, because leases tend to be anywhere between 5 and 25 years in length. Most commercial leases are 'insuring and repairing', which means the tenant is responsible for everything for the duration of their lease so, unlike with residential buy to let, you have no on-going maintenance or repair bills. With these longer leases, you may also be able to set periodical automatic rent increases at the start, making it easier for you to plan ahead.

In terms of natural increase in capital value, assuming you don't make any improvements, commercial properties don't tend to rise at the same rate as residential homes, mainly because of the difference in demand. As the population increases, more and more homes are needed, but with businesses always looking to consolidate, there's not the same proportional rise in demand. However, yields for commercial properties are usually slightly higher on average than for standard residential single-unit lets, which makes up for that, to a certain extent. And, because the leases are longer, you don't have the same risk of void periods as you do with residential.

What should I buy?

As with any property investment, you need to be very careful about what you buy and the type of business your tenant is in because the commercial market is much more vulnerable to economic fluctuations - people don't need warehouses and office blocks in the same way that they need a roof over their heads. That being said, there is currently a lot of evidence that UK commercial property is a fairly safe bet.

'In June 2013, Investec Wealth, the wealth manager, announced it was moving its discretionary clients to an overweight holding in UK commercial property over the next 12 months, with the best opportunities outside London.'
FT.com, August 2013

The FT also reported that construction output levels are still very low and suggested that the supply of new commercial premises is likely to be extremely limited over the next 5 years.

And in July 2014, Savills Research UK Commercial reported:

'UK commercial activity expands at sharpest pace in four months.'

Because of the lack of new build office space, it seems that there is certainly money to be made in buying 'tired' existing office premises and bringing them up to a sharp, modern standard. As with any renovation project, you will need to invest a good amount of capital, but the uplift in value, combined with the rent you should be able to charge the right tenant, should more than compensate you.

Probably the most common kind of commercial investment for private individuals in the past has been a shop with residential accommodation above, because the letting of larger office buildings and industrial units is more complex and demands more specialist knowledge. But I have a couple of warehouses that I've let for a few years now, without any trouble, and I'd suggest it's well worth looking at all commercial opportunities in your area that fall within your affordability.

You will need to spend some time understanding the commercial market and find specialists in commercial financing, surveying and letting to advise you. I'd recommend investing locally, as you'll already have an awareness of the shape of the economy. Just as the demand for residential rental varies from area to area, so certain commercial propositions will be better than others, depending on local market forces and future plans.

Bear in mind...
- In terms of financing, you'll probably need to invest more capital than you would in a similarly-priced residential property as LTVs are usually a maximum of 65%
- Banks will generally put some restrictive covenants on commercial lending
- It can be very difficult to remove a tenant during their tenancy
- Roughly half of all new businesses fail within the

first three years (you'll find a variety of figures quoted by different sources, but 50% seems to be a fair approximation) so check your tenant out thoroughly before agreeing the lease terms
- If you want to refinance, the banks will take into account the quality of the current tenant when valuing the property and its lease

I've talked here about buying and holding a commercial property but there is also the option of turning your investment around more quickly – although that's less common. You could simply improve the property and the value of the lease and re-sell, but when yields are perceived as generally good and you can factor in rent increases, why not hold on to it. If you buy right, you could be sitting on a very profitable piece of prime real estate!

Land banking (via companies)

I'm going to be brief here, because land banking is purely speculative – it's like gambling. As with investing overseas, which I'm going to cover in the next chapter, it's only for those with money to spare.

The concept is that you either buy a specific plot that you own yourself or, as is more common, you form part of 'consortium' that funds the purchase of a larger piece of land. The land doesn't have planning permission and has been selected because someone believes that it will be possible to secure planning for a significant development – either residential or commercial – in the future.

There are a lot of land banking companies offering plots for investment, where your capital is usually tied up for an absolute minimum of 5 years. There's no certain medium to long-term outcome and, because all you have is a piece of unused land, you're not getting any income in the meantime. I don't consider that a sensible investment because if capital growth isn't assured, you need to be getting a decent monthly return.

"Plan and prepare for the future, because that's where you're going to spend the rest of your life."

Mark Twain

KEY NOTES

- Buy in a location where the infrastructure and local economy are sound, and local services are within easy reach

- Character properties or homes with distinguishing features tend to sell on well

- No matter how good the purchase deal, make sure the investment stacks up on the rental front and gives you an on-going return that's at least as good as you could get from a savings account or other more traditional investment

- Consider commercial property but bear in mind you'll need specialist advice – see Chapter 9

- Steer clear of land-banking companies!

Chapter 7

Investing overseas

Investing overseas is an odd proposition. It's probably the most risky type of property investment you can make and the most difficult to get right. Ironically, it's the people who are least prepared and least equipped to make the decision to invest overseas who often end up doing it. They get blinded by impressive marketing and sales patter, jump in and usually find themselves stuck with something that bears no resemblance to the deal they thought they were getting; in the worst cases, losing all their capital.

It's not a reliable income strategy, because the associated management costs - not to mention the cost of you travelling to the property when necessary – tend to be so high, so if you're considering an overseas investment, it should be based on capital appreciation. And that's something of an issue, because projecting how a relatively new market is likely to perform over the coming years is very tricky.

The dream
Most people who are interested in property and have money to invest have been targeted at some point with overseas 'opportunities', so

you've probably seen the dream yourself. It's the promise that if you put your money into land and/or new developments in up-and-coming 'hotspots', you'll be able to sell in a few years for a huge profit and benefit from great rental returns in the meantime. Often, the projected rental returns come with a 'guarantee' and there may also be a financing option on offer that means you can make all this money in return for very little investment of your own capital.

The brochures, scale models and locations make the properties look glamorous and high quality. Impressive facts and figures about huge demand and a stream of locals or tourists begging for just this kind of accommodation will be forthcoming and the focus will be on the dazzling potential returns.

The reality

The success stories and instances where investors have really made a lot of money in overseas markets are few and far between. That's because it takes a lot of effort and expertise to be able to identify a market that's right at the start of its growth spurt and, to get the best returns, you need to make your investment at a very early stage. And when a market is at that early a stage in its cycle, you're unlikely to be able to secure financing, so it means you'll be funding your investment 100% yourself. That's a heck of a risk to take.

The people who take these risks spend a lot of time on planes, visiting countries, meeting and building relationships with local developers and officials. It really does take money to make money overseas and I'm confident in saying that all the truly successful overseas investors have also lost a good deal of money. But, because they're well capitalised, they can afford to gamble and when they win big it more than makes up for any losses along the way.

These are the people who are selling deals to you. By the time they've secured planning permission and put financing schemes in place, it's been two or three years since they made their own investment and the initial opportunity for big profit has passed.

So when you're presented with something that looks almost too good to be true, you have to ask yourself: if it's such a great deal and the profits are so certain, why aren't the developers keeping it for themselves? Because they can make a lot more money from selling to naïve investors at inflated purchase prices that no local person or large investment institution would dream of paying – that's the reality much of the time.

Financing schemes usually consist of some kind of personal loan that is secured on an existing asset, probably your own home, and the 'guaranteed' rental returns will be fixed in some way, certainly built into the price you're paying. When the period of that guarantee comes to an end, most return slump. Then, because all the virtually identical units have been sold to investors under the same investment principle, you find everyone wants to sell at the same time. The result is a flood of property to a market where locals can't afford to pay inflated prices and other investors want new builds, not second hand properties in a location that's yesterday's news.

I realise I'm painting a biased and sceptical picture, but I honestly have yet to see an overseas deal that meets my own risk/reward criteria. Investing in so-called 'emerging' markets is not something I've done myself, or would ever do.

But if you think it's worth taking the risk for a potentially excellent return that can't be matched by any UK-based property investment, read on.

Types of opportunity

There are three main types of investment you can make:

Land

Buying land in an area where the market cycle is in its absolute infancy and being as sure as you can be that there will be an economic infrastructure in the near future to support it is how you'll make the best return. As I mentioned above, it does carry high risk, because you'll probably be buying before planning permission has been secured and will more than likely need to buy the land for cash.

You can make smaller investments by buying a small piece of land on your own or a larger plot as part of a consortium; if you have a lot of capital, you can enter into larger ventures. For that, you would need to take the time to research and secure local business partners, and that's a major investment that very few people would enter into on their own.

The investment plan is usually for a lump-sum return, either within a couple of years, through selling the land at a significant mark-up, or in three to five years, by building it out and selling the development. Some developers choose to keep an interest, either by retaining the freehold of the whole site and/or ownership of an income-generating asset, such as a restaurant or hotel.

Pro: Because you're getting in at a very early stage, there is the potential for excellent short to medium-term profit.
Con: It's very high risk and capital intensive.

Off-plan
This is probably the most common type of opportunity you'll be offered. You're usually investing at the stage where planning permission has been granted and the architects' designs, scale models and artists' impressions have been created. Work may or may not have started on the development.

There are a few things to be very wary of. Firstly, what you're looking at is an idealistic, sanitised version of the end result. And this is just one reason why I don't like buying off-plan – I like to be able to look at and around a property and see exactly what I'm putting my money into. Secondly, planning permission has not always been fully granted, so make sure you find that out, or you may be investing into a pipe dream. Thirdly, there's the timescale. Building projects invariably take longer than planned, so your rental returns are unlikely to start rolling in when you expect them to.

Finally, and most significantly, there are the projected returns themselves. The promised capital gain is likely to be the main focus of the sales pitch, hotly followed by rental returns, but what are these projections based on? You're usually buying into a new market which, as I've already covered, will more than likely have already had its initial growth spurt, so don't be fooled by any of the historical price growth figures – they're fairly meaningless for you.

Pro: None that I can think of!
Con: You're buying an idea, nothing tangible. At least when you're buying land, you can see the ground!

Existing developments

This is where you can see exactly what it is you're buying. It may be almost finished, recently completed or a second-hand sale. The 'red flag' with this is the fact that it's available at all. Generally speaking, when an overseas opportunity is genuinely that good, the whole development is sold at the off-plan stage. Developers want to get their money back as soon as possible, so it's highly unlikely any of them would deliberately hold back on the release of units until they're fully built.

And by the time a development is complete, the market cycle has usually already slowed right down or plateaued entirely, which means you've missed the boat as far as decent capital growth is concerned. I'd suggest the only people who should be buying at this stage are those who want a holiday home for themselves that they can rent out the rest of the year to keep things ticking over money-wise. It's unlikely to be a financially rewarding move or a viable investment opportunity for the pure investor.

Pro: You can at least see the property as it really is.
Con: The market has probably already emerged and shaken itself dry, so returns are unlikely to be worth the effort and cost involved in buying overseas.

The long and short of overseas investing, in my opinion, is that it's only for the well-capitalised and well-connected speculative investor - or the holiday home buyer. Yes, the potential returns if you get in early enough may be better than anything you could achieve in the UK, but you also run a far greater risk of losing your investment.

However, you may still think it's worth a go, in the interests of diversifying your portfolio and having somewhere you could holiday yourself. In that case, there are a few key things I'd suggest you look at very carefully before you take the plunge.

Be very wary of...

The proposed exit strategy

Generally speaking, units in overseas developments are sold to the same kind of investor: someone who wants a decent lump-sum return in around 3 years. I'm always amazed that it occurs to so few people to question who, exactly, is going to be there to buy what they're trying to sell. As I've already said, locals either can't afford to buy or don't want what's being sold and other investors want the latest new build, not a second-hand unit. For the very few buyers who might be interested, they have such a choice that the price can be driven right down.

A very good example of this is the coastal apartment craze in Spain in the early 2000s, when investors snapped up units on the new developments that were springing up by the sea. And yes, a few lucky people who'd got in right at the start managed to make a decent return. But by the time most people came to sell, the realisation dawned that there was no resale market as investors had moved on to the new 'hotspots' - Cyprus, Romania, Cape Verdi... Spain was old news and they'd be lucky if they simply broke even because the market was flooded with identical properties that nobody wanted to buy. Many have simply been left with an unwanted holiday apartment that costs them money every year.

So the first questions you should ask when you're looking for a lump sum return is: who's going to buy it, why, and how are they going to be able to pay what I want for it?

Forecasted returns

You'll be tempted by some excellent-sounding returns, but make sure you ask what they're based on. What happened in the previous couple of years is irrelevant, as there's no guarantee that kind of growth will continue. Just as when you're investing in a new area in the UK, you need to be asking questions about the local economy and infrastructure: are there currently or are there plans in place to build schools and shops, are businesses moving into the area and does it have decent transport links?

Guaranteed returns

Approach guaranteed returns with a healthy scepticism! If a developer is offering to guarantee a certain level of rental income for the property (usually for the first year or possibly 18 months), it suggests to me that they're not confident in the market. If it really was an excellent property for which there was huge demand, why would they need the 'carrot' of a guarantee to tempt you to buy? And they're not doing it out of the goodness of their hearts, so be aware you're paying for it somewhere along the line, either in the purchase price or the maintenance charge.

Price

Where have they got this from? It's quite tricky to accurately value a new build in the UK, and we have a very established and secure economy and property market. Trying to put a definite value on a new kind of accommodation that's being offered in a very young market is virtually impossible. The developer or agent will have their own team of surveyors and will put forward all kinds of evidence to support the price, but it's highly advisable to get your own, independent second opinion.

Legal and financial professionals

The opportunity is usually packaged nicely so you don't have to 'worry' about anything. The developer/agent will put you in touch with their finance people and legal team who are well acquainted with the way this deal is structured and have all the right contacts on the ground to ensure everything goes smoothly. You may even be assigned a personal consultant who will keep you up to date every step of the way.

We're back to the old, 'if it looks too good to be true…' Companies selling investments want to make it as easy as possible for you to part with your money because they're in it to make a big profit themselves. So, while you shouldn't have to 'worry', you absolutely must do your due diligence. Have your own independent financial advisor or mortgage broker look at the financing and instruct your own legal representative, ideally one from a firm that has offices and staff trained in both the UK and whichever country you're looking at investing in.

Get on a plane

You'll probably be told this is an ideal 'armchair investment', where you can make a lot of money for very little effort yourself, and I simply don't believe that's possible. I'm a firm believer in gut instinct and I would never buy a property unseen in an area I hadn't visited. You get a feeling for a place, so if you truly believe the opportunity you're being offered is a great one, spend a few hundred pounds on seeing the plot or the development for yourself.

In summary

You'll have gathered I'm not a fan of investing overseas. Yes, it is possible to succeed and make a lot of money, but if you're going to do that effectively it's pretty much a full-time job. And that's not what about making investments to secure your financial future is about.

Really look at all the costs involved and work out whether the returns look good enough to risk buying in a largely untested market, with a legal system, language and culture you may not understand, a long way from home. And when you're calculating profit, make sure you talk to someone who's a financial expert in overseas investing, because there are likely to be tax implications in bringing money back to the UK, not to mention the risk of exchange rate fluctuations. The returns that have been dangled under your nose may not be quite as attractive when you look at what you're actually likely to net.

As far as I'm concerned, the UK offers such a wide range of ways in which you can make money from property, there's no reason to go to the trouble or take on the risk of buying abroad. We have a solid economy that supports one of the most stable and secure property markets in the world and there are a plethora of opportunities very close to your doorstep.

KEY NOTES

- The only reason the returns are higher in emerging markets is that the risks are higher

- Approach any company selling you an opportunity with a healthy skepticism!

- If you decide to buy off-plan or an existing property, go for something unique, e.g. a one-off design, a penthouse or a corner apartment with a larger balcony

- Tourist and investment trends can come and go, particularly when you're talking about 'emerging markets', so make sure there's a solid local economy and demand to support the exit from your investment

- Use your own, independent team of legal and financial advisors, who have offices both in the UK and in the country in question

- Spend time with an overseas tax expert and understand the implications of bringing money back into the UK

PART THREE:

PUTTING IT INTO PRACTICE

Chapter 8

What kind of investor are you?

Understanding something about the array of property investment options available to you is one thing; choosing which will suit you is quite another. I've heard it said many times that not everyone is suited to property as an investment vehicle, but I don't agree. While not everyone can necessarily make a success of building and managing a portfolio of HMOs, property is such a varied form of investment that you're bound to find a path that works for you.

All that being said, assuming you're planning to take my advice and source your own properties to build a portfolio – whether big or small - you need to have the right personality and skill set, an appropriate attitude to risk, sufficient time available and a decent amount of money to invest. If you'd rather let someone else handle the acquisition and management of property assets for you, then your own skills, experience and time needn't come into the equation. Mind you, I hope I've already been clear that if you'd rather take the hands-off approach, you do run the risk of ending up with properties that aren't necessarily going to deliver what you want and need and your profits certainly won't be as great.

"An investment in knowledge pays the best interest."

Benjamin Franklin

Your financial position

I'm starting with this because the amount of capital you have and your ability to borrow will obviously govern what kind of investments you can make.

Property investing nowadays is a fairly capital-intensive business. With pretty much every other form of investment, you put your money in at the start and that's that. The capital value might go up and you may get regular interest payments or dividends, or the capital value might drop, but it's highly unlikely you'll be expected to top up your initial investment.

Property, on the other hand needs maintaining. Even if it's freshly renovated or a new build, there will still be things that need doing down the line. If you have void periods, where the property is un-let, you still have to pay the mortgage and possibly other bills, such as council tax and utility bills. If you have HMOs, you'll probably be responsible for on-going general maintenance and if it's a leasehold property there will be a service charge and ground rent to consider. Yes, you work all these costs into your budget and ensure the rental income is such that you're not left out of pocket every month, but you need to prepare yourself and put money aside for the larger jobs that come along every 5, 10 or 15 years, such as new boilers, kitchens, bathrooms, carpets and redecoration. So you need to plan and budget ahead.

Buy to let mortgages: On average, a lender will want to see a surveyor's rental valuation equal to or greater than 125% of the mortgage repayment amount. For example:

Purchase price	£200,000
Mortgage at 75% LTV	£150,000
Monthly interest-only mortgage at 5%	£625
Surveyor's valuation must be at least	£781

Note that, while the mortgage is based primarily on the rental income, the lender will also want to see your personal income at a certain level, usually £25,000 or more.

And at the start, there's the initial deposit and purchase costs for each property. Buy to let mortgages at reasonable rates will probably be at no more than 75-80% loan to value (LTV), so you'll need enough capital available to cover 20-25% of the purchase price for the deposit, plus:

- Stamp Duty Land Tax (likely to be 1% for the average buy to let; 3% over £250,000)
- around 1% of the purchase price for all your other fees and services

- potentially tens of thousands for renovation and refurbishment.

If you've researched your purchase and the market properly, all that money should represent simply an initial and then further investment – it's not as though you're losing it; you're just 'moving' it from the bank into bricks and mortar....which brings me nicely on to my next point...

What's your attitude to risk and debt?

If you're buying property at the current UK average of approaching around £200,000, you can easily find yourself with mortgage debt of £160k and £50k of your own capital tied up in each property (80% LTV, plus assuming some refurbishment). If you're building a portfolio, you will quickly pass the million pound mark in terms of borrowing and you are responsible for making the mortgage repayments on that debt every month.

The common perception is that property is low risk, 'safe as houses', but in the investment market it's regarded as medium risk. Prices can go down and if you don't keep up the repayments on the mortgage, you could be in danger of losing your investment entirely. That being said, the likelihood of it actually happening to you is incredibly small, unless you made a truly terribly error in judgment on purchase.

The key to successful investment is taking a **calculated** risk and a great benefit of investing in property, versus something like the stock market, is that it's within your power to minimise that risk. Letting a property for a level of rent that covers the associated costs each month and gives you some profit on top means you shouldn't ever have to subsidise the mortgage repayments – your borrowing is 'good debt' rather than 'bad debt'. And as long as you did your research properly before you bought it and maintain it well, you shouldn't have any nasty surprises down the line.

The caveat is that you do need to cover yourself, just in case. Never spend all your profit; keep a proportion aside so that if the worst should happen and you end up with an extended period without a tenant or an unexpectedly large bill for work on the property, the money's there.

Planning for the best but preparing for the worst is simply a sensible way to approach business and although property investment carries risk, I would certainly say that well-planned property investment is less risky than many other options for your money. Yes, prices can fluctuate and demand can change, but buildings are flexible things. You can change the type of tenant, type of let and the way the accommodation is laid out (subject to local council regulations and planning permission, of course), letting for as long as you want or need, then refinancing or selling when the time is right.

So how's it all sounding to you so far? Hopefully good, but if you have any doubts, please take some time to think about what you're looking at getting yourself into. I'm sure I've said it before, but I'm going to say it again: I love property – and I've got loads of mortgage debt! I'm really happy with my investment plans and I have good systems in place for my property business so I'm confident that on the risk:reward ratio, reward is winning by a mile.

But that's me; you might feel differently. And there's no point in leveraging yourself to the hilt with an income-generating portfolio that makes you good money month on month if it also gives you anxiety and sleepless nights because you're so worried about how much you owe the bank and how you'll manage if all the tenants leave and five properties turn out to need new roofs. So have a good think.

More about you...

Much of life and business is about selling, negotiation and problem solving, and successful property investment demands that you're good at all three. In short, you have to be good with people: intuitive, diplomatic and personable.

To a greater or lesser extent, depending on your investment strategy, you have to be able to build relationships with estate agents (after you've worked out which are going to be the most useful to you); present yourself to vendors in the best light and negotiate purchases; work effectively with legal and financial advisors; attract, screen and manage tenants and their problems; deal with contractors....

all of which you'll be far more successful at if you're a 'people person' with great communication skills.

There are certainly people operating in the property investment industry who are anything but diplomatic and personable – they're simply skilled at persuasion and manipulation – and who are nonetheless perceived as successful. Those kinds of people tend to either do a series of one-off deals so that they're working with new people each time or act as the 'charming' face of a company but get other people to actually handle the business. They enjoy bouts of short-term success but usually also suffer big losses periodically and many have been declared bankrupt more than once or had their companies put into administration.

But when you're making an investment for your long-term financial security, you can't afford to be like that, especially if you're going to trust other people to handle the various different aspects of your portfolio and financial affairs – something I'll come on to in detail in the next chapter.

How are your business and admin skills?

I've said already that if you have a buy to let property portfolio, you have a property business. If you're investing in a series of single-let properties that an agent is letting and managing for you, you won't have too much administration to handle yourself, but if you're carrying out renovation, self-build or building a portfolio of HMOs, there is a huge amount of paperwork and other jobs that need to be carried out.

To give you an idea, here are some of the main administrative and business elements of investing in property:

(a) Regardless of how you let, refurbish and sell or build, you will need to be concerned with:
- Initial wealth / investment planning with a suitable financial advisor
- Investment research / documentation
- Legal and financial purchase paperwork
- Survey report
- On-going bookkeeping, tax returns and capital gains matters

(b) If you refurbish:
- All of (a)
- Quotes and bills for refurbishment
- Dealing with the local council for building regulations compliance and planning permission, as necessary, particularly so if the property is to be an HMO
- Engagement and management of contractors
- Receipts, warranties, etc for work

(c) If you're having an agent manage your buy to lets for you:
- All of (a)
- Possibly all of (b)

- Ensuring the property is health & safety compliant (installing smoke detectors, correct ventilation, etc.)
- Gaining gas safe, electrical and energy performance certificates
- Possibly furnishing the property
- Sourcing a suitable agent
- Agreeing tenancy terms
- Signing off larger maintenance and repair jobs
- Checking monthly rent has been received

(d) If you're self-managing a single let:
- All of (a)
- Possibly all of (b)
- Ensuring the property is health & safety compliant (installing smoke detectors, correct ventilation, etc.)
- Gaining gas safe, electrical and energy performance certificates
- Possibly furnishing the property
- Advertising for, interviewing and referencing tenants
- The tenancy agreement
- Checking tenants in and out and taking or organising an inventory
- Protecting the tenant's deposit
- Collecting and chasing rent, as necessary
- Dealing with tenant and property issues
- Rent reviews, renewals and re-lets
- Maintaining the property and liaising with contractors – as

well as building a good relationship with them
- Organising annual gas safety checks and periodical electrical and fire safety checks

If you're self-managing an HMO:
- All of (a), (b) and (d)
- Possibly getting the property licensed, depending on local authority requirements (definitely, if the property has 5 or more people living over 3 or more storeys)
- Several time over the amount of paperwork and probably maintenance as for a single let
- Paying council tax and probably utility bills and a TV license
- Organising cleaning services
- Managing a team. As your portfolio grows, you will certainly need to take on some staff – assuming you don't want to run yourself into the ground! – so will encounter all the administration that comes with having employees.

If you decide to go into self-build and/or development, that's a small business turn-around in itself.

In consultation with your financial advisor or wealth manager, you may also be dealing with:
- Setting up and assuming directorship of a limited company
- Trusts
- Other tax-efficiency and inheritance planning

...the list goes on and the above is by no means exhaustive. There is a lot to do so, while you can learn as you go along, it's a great help if you've already had experience of running a business, no matter how small, and are very organised with a keen eye for detail.

You're also going to need to be self-motivated. Once you've been investing for a few years and have built a good local reputation, some deals will come to you but, for the most part, you need to go out there and find them for yourself. You've got to be keen enough to really make a success of your property investments to keep looking for ways to refine your portfolio and make it as profitable as possible, without compromising on quality, care or your legal obligations. And nobody's going to be there making you do it!

How much time do you have?

This is a big factor in deciding what kind of investments will suit you.

I've chosen to dedicate most of my time to property investment because I'm sure it will pay dividends in the future. However, I'm in my early 40s and have been investing seriously for the past nine years; you may be in a different position and if you're coming to this later in life, or you already have a busy job that you love, you may not want to dedicate as much time as I have.

To build a portfolio, particularly an income-generating one, the first few years are very hard work. If you're taking on any building work - from even minor refurbishment to a new build – you can't underestimate the amount of time you'll need to dedicate to the project. If you choose to self-manage your buy to let properties, you not only need to set time aside for carrying out admin and viewings, but also accept that you'll need to be 'on call' for any problems or things that need your attention at short notice.

Again, I'll say that I think the hard work in the early days is well worth the time investment, because of the financial benefits, but you might feel differently.

What's your time worth?

A big part of deciding what kind of investor you want to be comes down to the value you place on your own time, both financially and emotionally. Broadly speaking, you'll make more gross profit the more hands on you are, but your time has a value and, while that might sound like an obvious thing to say, it always amazes me how many people forget about it.

You'll have seen people on 'Grand Designs' and 'Property Ladder' talking about the equity they've got or the profits they've made at the end of six months, a year, two years….but what about all the time they've spent on the project themselves, often working very late into the night, not going on holiday, sacrificing time with friends and family, taking time off from their 'day jobs'…? I often look at them when all the work's finished, they're exhausted and I think,

"Was it worth it?". Yes, it costs money to pay project managers and get contractors in to carry out every job, and I understand that sometimes people simply don't have the money in the bank to pay someone else, but a lot of the time it really is a false economy.

So think what else you could be doing with your time and what that's worth to you. It might be working on souring a new, profitable property deal; focusing more on your existing career; spending more time with friends and family; taking more holidays; pursuing sporting interests or other hobbies...all those things will have a value, whether monetary or emotional and you need to work out which tasks benefit you more.

There will be certain things, such as paperwork, bookkeeping and dealing with tenant problems, that you're not all that good at or that you don't feel confident about handling yourself. Now, you could train yourself to be better at those things – or you could simply employ someone else to do them for you. I'm a firm believer in playing to your strengths and find that investing my time in becoming more skilled at things for which I already have an aptitude is a far better choice than struggling through, trying to get to grips with something that doesn't come naturally.

"To avoid your strengths and to focus on your weaknesses isn't a sign of diligent humility. It is almost irresponsible. By contrast the most responsible, the most challenging, and the most honorable thing to do is face

up to the strength potential inherent in your talents and then find ways to realize it."

Donald O. Clifton, Psychologist

For me, the decision about how to manage my property investments comes down to three things:

1. Much of the admin and management is repetitive and can be irritating and quite disruptive to any daily routine. Some people like letting properties and managing tenants – a number of my clients find they get a great deal of satisfaction from having a system that works and making sure their tenants are happy – but that doesn't suit my temperament or personality.

2. I want to make sure my choice of investment improves the quality of my life and helps me realise my goals, one of which is to spend as much time as I can with my family, either at home or abroad. In order for that to happen, I need a system that can keep things running smoothly, whether I'm there every day or not; a business that continues to be profitable even when I'm in Spain for a fortnight!

3. I'm at my most effective when I'm helping others and finding new deals – those are the things that excite me and bring me the greatest financial rewards over the long-term. My time is best spent negotiating and mentoring; I can't afford to be spending the majority of the day in the office or

attending personally to the management of my properties…

…which is why I employ other people to run my portfolio.

Your own business or someone else's?

So, in building a portfolio of investment properties, you have four choices:

1. Source, refurbish, let and manage properties yourself
2. Source properties yourself and employ people to let and manage them for you, building up a small property business
3. Source properties yourself and hand them over to a 3rd party letting agent
4. Pay an investment company or property 'sourcer' to find deals for you and then either manage them yourself or through a letting agent

I would never recommend option 4, because you're quite honestly paying through the nose for an investment that's out of your hands. As I said in the last chapter, I'm not a fan of using other people to find deals for you. Property sourcers simply take an up-front fee and have no financial interest in how your investment performs and investment companies usually play with the figures to make you think you're getting property at better value than you really are, then take a disproportionately large fee for their services.

Option 3 is worthwhile if you're going to be away from your investment area for much of the time or if you only have a couple of investments and don't want or feel able to manage them yourself. If you have a larger portfolio, you will end up paying more in fees than it would cost you to employ your own small team.

Option 1 is where you're likely to start out with your first couple of properties, and I'd always recommend getting your hands dirty at the beginning so that you really understand what's needed and what kind of person and skills it takes to be a good property manager. But, as I said earlier in the book, when you get to 5+ properties it can easily become a full-time job and that usually defeats the purpose of making the investments in the first place!

By far the best route to take, in my opinion, is Option 2, but that does demand good business, managerial and interpersonal skills. By building your own small business you keep much better control over income and expenditure; you have a dedicated team working only for you; you can tailor the staffing and business structure perfectly to your choice of type of investment properties and it's very easy to scale up, as discussed in Chapter 5.

But having an in-house team is only part of the picture. If you're going to be successful in property investing you need the right advice and services on many different fronts...

Chapter 9

Get the best advice

While it's a fabulous investment vehicle, property really should come with a warning, because it is a potential minefield. You need to make sure you buy the right things; mortgage rules, criteria and rates change regularly; your properties need to be bought and let out in a way that is legally right for you and your circumstances; there's a huge amount of legislation around buy to let that seems to be constantly updated or amended; you need to make sure management and maintenance problems are resolved quickly and effectively; any refurbishment or building work must be appropriate and approved; you need to be compliant with bookkeeping and tax regulations – in short, there's a lot you need to get right.

And you can't possibly be an expert in all those areas, so the very best thing you can do for your investment business is tap into the knowledge, skills and resources of the people who *are* experts in their own specific fields and surround yourself with some really good advisors, suppliers and associates.

I use the services of more than 25 different people on a regular basis. They're all very good at what they do, which enables me to acquire properties efficiently and for the business to run with minimal daily input from me. I think of these people as my 'team':

- Wealth Manager
- Specialist Property Lawyers
- Independent Mortgage Broker
- Accountant
- Bookkeeper
- Estate Agents
- Property Manager
- Lettings Negotiators
- Project Manager for refurbishments
- Maintenance team and specialist contractors
- Personal Assistant
- Business Manager

No matter how intuitive you are, you won't always pick the right people the first time and I've made a number of changes since I began investing. As you get to know your investments better, you'll realise exactly what skills and expertise you need and be able to refine your team accordingly. I've worked with most of my advisors, suppliers and employees for a number of years now and am happy that it's a very strong line-up.

A really important thing to bear in mind when you're interviewing or assessing the suitability of people you're considering working with is how much you actually like them. A lot of people say that they're not bothered about that – it's much more important that the person is good at their job – but I disagree. We're not talking about a one-off deal where you're never going to have to deal with that person again, we're talking about finding a number of people you can trust to help you invest in the best way for you and help make your future as financially secure as possible. These are people you'll be working with on a regular basis and I have no desire to work with people I don't like.

If you don't like someone, you're unlikely to trust them and there's a high level of trust in what you're asking of your team. Surround yourself with people with whom you feel a natural rapport and don't be tempted to engage someone just because they've been highly recommended to you or have exceptional qualifications and experience. People tend to do more for you, make themselves more available and go the extra mile if they actually like you, so build solid relationships, based on genuine trust and respect, with people whose company you enjoy and it will pay dividends in your investment business.

"In the end, all business operations can be reduced to three words: people, product, and profits. Unless you've got a good team, you can't do much with the other two."

Lee Iacocca, Businessman & Former CEO of Chrysler

**All professionals giving you financial advice MUST be properly qualified and regulated by the Financial Services Authority (FSA) and anyone giving you legal advice should be suitably qualified and regulated by The Law Society and the Solicitors Regulation Authority (SRA) (or the Council of Licensed Conveyancers (CLC)).

Wealth Manager

One of the most important things to consider is how property fits alongside your other financial interests. A Wealth Manager will look at all your financial affairs – earnings, investments, trusts, etc. – and work to ensure they're all complementing each other to achieve your investment goals and are tax efficient.

You can engage a wealth management firm or take advantage of your bank's wealth management service but try to make sure you're working with someone who either invests in property themselves or already has a number of property investor clients. It'll short-cut your discussions and they're likely to have researched the subject very well indeed.

Take your investment objectives and personal financial statement (see Chapter 1) along to your meeting, so that the Wealth Manager can get a clear picture of your current situation and what you want your financial future to look like. They can then help you decide the best way to structure your investments and, importantly, discuss whether property is even the best place for you to be putting your money. Although it's not terribly common, sometimes a person's existing financial situation and plans and needs for the future are better satisfied by another form of investment.

Importantly, a Wealth Manager can also help you with inheritance planning. Too many people invest in property so they have something to leave to their children, without realising that it can be one of the least tax-efficient ways to pass on money. You'll need to amend your Will and may need to set up Trusts – it's a complex area, and requires specialist advice.

The best advice certainly doesn't come cheap, but in the long run it will save you many, many times over what it costs you.

As well as being FSA regulated, ideally they will also have the CISI Masters in Wealth Management (MCSI after their name).

Property tax specialist / accountant

Wealth management firms are usually able to give you tax advice and handle your accounts, but you must make sure that you've had a proper discussion with someone who is a property tax expert. Your property investment plans will impact your current tax situation - and vice versa - and a specialist will be able to advise you how to invest and set up and run your property business in the most tax-efficient way.

As well as qualifying under the Association of Chartered Certified Accountants (ACCA), your tax advisor should also be a member of the Chartered Institute of Taxation (CTA).

Bookkeeper

You may want to try keeping your own books to start with, but I would suggest that unless you've already got bookkeeping experience and have thoroughly discussed with your tax advisor how to organize your affairs, it's far better to hand over this job to someone who's used to working with property investors. Quite apart form the technicalities of what to put where, the admin can mount up and it's unlikely to be the best use of your time. Bookkeepers needn't be expensive and, as with so many of the tasks you'll end up delegating, it's well worth the investment.

Mortgage broker / IFA

Your mortgage broker can make or break a deal. You're looking for someone who understands exactly what you're aiming for and appreciates that things often need to happen quickly. Make sure they're independent (i.e. can access all mortgage products in the market) and have worked in the investment market, specifically buy to let, for a number of years, as they're likely to have established relationships with buy to let and HMO specialist lenders.

I'd never attempt to find a mortgage myself by going direct to different lenders, for three key reasons:

1. It can be incredibly time-consuming and I'm not a mortgage expert.
2. Good brokers usually have access to mortgage products that aren't publicised – you only know they're there if you ask about them, and if you don't know they're there…!
3. As an individual, trying to contact lenders to progress an application can be an incredibly frustrating experience and you're unlikely to have any luck moving it along quickly. An effective broker will be able to access the right people and push your application through.

Having a good broker will really add value to your investment portfolio. Being well financed will mean you'll not only be able to act quickly on deals, but also get better deals and therefore be more profitable, and a good broker will always make sure you're one step ahead by periodically reviewing your mortgages and advising you of new, upcoming products that might be more suitable.

If you're looking at self-build or commercial investments, you may need to find a specialist broker for those. Financing for development projects is harder to come by so it's especially important you're working with someone who knows what they're doing and has a good track record.

Any person acting as a broker or making recommendations for your mortgage finance must have one or more of these qualifications: Certificate in Mortgage Advice (Cert MA); Certificate in Mortgage Advice and Practice (CeMAP) from the ifa School of Finance; Mortgage Advice and Practice Certificate (MAPC) from the CIB in Scotland.

Specialist property lawyer

Ideally, they should be buy to let specialists and have experience of dealing with whatever type of property investments you're planning to make. As with your broker, your legal representative can make the difference between a smooth and speedy transaction and a complete nightmare! You can instruct either a solicitor or a licensed conveyancer – both are qualified to handle property transactions – but one of the benefits of engaging a solicitor is that you can choose a firm that also has solicitors specialising in other areas of law. That means your legal representative can tap into the knowledge of colleagues for advice on things like tax planning, Wills, litigation, etc. and you may be able to keep all your legal affairs under one roof.

Some firms have specific case-progression departments; some solicitors/conveyancers will progress things themselves. Both have pros and cons - the important thing for you to establish is:

1. Are they happy to work to a timescale established at the start

(unforeseen circumstances aside)?

2. Will they update you regularly?

3. Will you be able to easily speak to the person directly dealing with your transaction?

You should also make sure that whoever you choose is happy to liaise with your broker/IFA and Wealth Manager to make sure the legal purchase structure of your investments is on track with your objectives. I know all this might sound like a lot to ask but this kind of legal professional does exist!

If the only property purchases you've made have been for your own home, there's every likelihood you've engaged a solicitor over the phone or online and have never actually met them. However, now that you're going to be making a number of investments over a number of years, take the time to go and meet a few different people face to face. Your lawyer's performance will be crucial to your success so make sure there's a good personal relationship and understanding from the start.

...and a legal lettings expert

Lettings legislation is constantly under review and it's virtually impossible for you to keep up to date with the latest changes and new laws and requirements yourself. If you're employing an in-house property manager, make sure they're experienced and qualified through the Association of Residential Letting Agents

(ARLA). That means they have to abide by a code of conduct and you can be confident they're fully briefed and up to date with regulations.

The alternative, if you're self-managing, is to retain the services of a legal lettings expert who can check that your tenancy agreements and management procedures are legally correct, advise and assist in serving notices to tenants and handle any eviction processes for you.

If you're intending to invest in HMOs or undertake any building work, the other person who can really help you stay on the right side of the law is a local planning expert. Planning regulations have a tendency to change rather quietly, so if you can build a relationship with a Chartered Town Planner, they can guide you and help you minimise the risk of falling foul of regulations.

Your own in-house team

I talked about building your own business and team of employees in the last chapter and the first person you should probably look to take on is a Property Manager. If you choose someone who is able and willing to take on other tasks while your portfolio is small, you can employ them full time from the outset. As I've already said, make sure they're ARLA qualified, or at least in training, and have some experience of handling tenants and property maintenance issues.

If you pick the right person, they should be able to manage other staff you might take on, such as a bookkeeper. Many of you reading this probably aren't planning on building a business as large as a lot of professional investors', so you'll probably be able to manage with just one or two people working for you. If, however, you do plan on building your own investment property empire, you're likely to have four or five employees. Either way, you will need to take some legal advice on employment law; your accountant will be able to help you set things up legally with HMRC.

Other service providers

Estate agents and contractors are the two main other types of service provider you'll need to build good relationships with. As I said in the last chapter, if you're going to be hands-on in building a portfolio of investment properties, you do need to be a 'people person' and making a good name for yourself as a reliable investor who does what they say you're going to do when you say you'll do it is particularly important here. These people work and live in the local area and you want the only words that get around to be good ones!

Estate agents

In most estate agencies these days there's at least one member of staff who understands about buying property purely as an investment and you need to make sure you're dealing with that person and that they understand exactly what you're looking for and why. Avoid agents who want to take your contact details before they've even asked what you're looking for – focus on the ones who actually want to have a conversation. You also want someone who knows the area and market well, so try to deal with senior negotiators or the branch manager, as they're more likely to be able to have a productive discussion.

Independent agents are usually owned and/or managed by people who have lived and worked in the area for quite some time. They're often on local boards and well connected, so can be a very useful source of information about upcoming properties and developments, planning and other investors who may be interested in partnering on projects.

Talk to the agents about your plans, show them you have your finances and legal representation in place, then view a few properties and explain exactly what's right and wrong, so they build up a picture of your ideal purchase. This is especially important if you're looking for properties suitable to reconfigure and let as HMOs. Contact and feedback are key; always view properties they recommend right away and keep them posted on what stage you're at in any transactions so they don't need to 'chase' you.

Ideally, you want to get to a position where you have two or three agents that understand exactly what you're looking for and know you'll act quickly and make sensible offers, so will call you as soon as they see a property that might be suitable. The quicker a sale can be agreed and completed, the sooner the agents get their money – you're an agent's dream! – so don't give them any reason not to want to have you at the top of their buyer list.

Agents MUST be members of The Property Ombudsman. Ideally, deal with agents who are Fellows of the National Association of Estate Agents (FNAEA) and/or the Royal Institution of Chartered Surveyors (FRICS).

Reliable contractors

Reliable contractors are worth their weight in gold – and then some. You need a team you can rely on for any refurbishment projects and then a team that can handle on-going maintenance. While you'll probably be able to use many of the same people, some contractors prefer to only handle larger projects and some only smaller ones, which is often the case with electricians and plumbers. The most important thing is that you hire the right people for each job - and make sure they're accredited by or a member of the relevant trade body or organisation and have their own insurance.

You might be lucky enough to find a general builder who already has a team of people he works with regularly; if not, do ask contractors whether they can make recommendations – i.e. does the plumber know a good electrician? The people you use for any refurbishments need to be able to work together – if they all have their own agendas, you can find projects stall or take longer than necessary because they're all blaming each other for not being able to get on to the next stage. Ideally, find a builder who is also prepared to project manage the work for you, then you can go through a clear plan at the start and pay him or her to make sure everything stays on track. That means you only have one person to liaise with, which can save you huge amounts of time and effort.

Your maintenance team – which will include a general handyman (worth their weight in gold!), plumber, electrician and cleaner – are people you're going to need to call on regularly, often at short notice, so do everything you can to make sure they respond to you quickly. A very good way of doing that is to pay them quickly when they invoice. Most – if not all – of these people will be self-employed and/or running small businesses and really can't afford to wait several weeks for payment, so will greatly appreciate you settling their bills right away.

You should be able to find good people by networking locally with other landlords and asking friends to recommend contractors they've used. You can also look on websites such as RatedPeople. com and mybuilder.com, where tradespeople have been rated on their work.

Building relationships with other investors and businesspeople

If you're seriously considering investing in property, you've probably come across some local 'meets' and been to one or two seminars, or at least heard about them. When I started out, I went to every one I could find, but I honestly didn't find them very helpful, mainly because they weren't focused enough on what I wanted to do and there were too many people simply trying to sell to me. That's not to say you might not get something from going along, but I'd suggest you're selective. Listen to a few speakers and then approach the ones that make the most sense to you. Talk about your thoughts and plans and you may find they're able to offer some valuable advice, but steer clear of the property sourcers and anyone offering 'discounted deals'.

I get lots of good ideas and advice from other investors and businesspeople, quite a few of whom I've found through my local landlords association and independent estate agents. Again, this comes down to being personable and business-minded and having good intuition. There are a heck of a lot of people out there in the industry that are trying to get something for nothing, but there are also a lot who agree that the more you give, the more you get, so share good ideas and good contacts and you'll find people will do the same in return.

And sometimes what you get from other people isn't necessarily what you expect. Countless times I've been at property events and ended up with a good tip, a new contact or an opportunity that's entirely unrelated to property. Holiday offers, car upgrades, a brilliant music teacher for one of my children, another kind of financial investment...all of these have saved me time and money, and I've made a lot of good friends as well.

Property can feel like quite an isolated business if you don't make the effort to build relationships and if you don't gel with your professional advisors, it can all feel like very hard work, no matter how good they are at their job. So I'll say it again: seek out the best advisors but make sure you also like and trust them. And if you have the personality and approach that they like in return, you'll find it much easier to gain and retain the best advice, service and support.

"The richest people in the world look for and build networks. Everyone else looks for work."

Robert Kiyosaki

KEY NOTES

- Only work with people you like and trust

- Make your first port of call a Wealth Manager, who can help you put together a solid investment plan

- Choose professional advisors who either invest in property themselves or have existing clients that do

- Seek out estate agents that understand about buying and letting property as an investment

- Always do what you say you're going to do, when you say you'll do it, and pay your contractors and other suppliers on time

- Network with other investors and businesspeople

Chapter 10

Summary: Where & how to start investing

Your question now is probably: "Right, where do I start?"

So, going back to the beginning, the first thing you need to do is look at your current pension provision and see how your financial future looks today. Are you happy with your projections and, more importantly, are you confident that what you've been told about how various funds and investments will mature is reliable information and advice? Map out a best and a worst-case scenario.

If you haven't done so already, review Chapter 1 and put together a financial statement, then write down what you want your financial future to look like, stating how much you need, why and by when – and what you want your life to be like as well. That will give both you and your Wealth Manager or financial advisor a solid place to start planning your investments. Don't forget, with the announcement about pension reforms in July 2014, came an assurance that free, impartial advice would also be available to everyone affected, so perhaps that might be an interesting place to begin, but I would certainly consult your own wealth advisor before taking any action, as the free advice on offer is likely to be quite limited.

Your 'wealth profile', as I'll call it, needs to be considered alongside the kind of investor you are:

- What's your attitude to risk and debt?
- What are your personal and business strengths and skills and how do they suit the requirements of hands-on property investing?
- How much time do you have available? It's really important you think about this in the context of your family life and discuss it with your family because, as I've said, if you want to be completely hands-on, it can be pretty much a full-time job.

Putting your finances, investment goals and personal capabilities together will enable you and your Wealth Manager or financial advisor to come up with a suitable investment plan.

If you choose to go down the 'active' investor route...

...then this is where the real work starts and you need to find some good people to work with, as outlined in the last chapter. Start networking locally with property groups and estate agents and get to know the market.

Investing successfully in buy to lets demands that you know the local sales and rental markets very well, as covered in Chapter 4 – and there's some more detailed information on market analysis in **'HMO PROPERTY SUCCESS'**, which I'd highly recommend you read if you've decided to invest in income-generating properties. You'll need to be able to estimate as accurately as possible all your initial costs, on-going income and expenditure and assess the financial viability of properties. Then you need to plan how to transform them from what you've purchased into the type of let that will be most profitable in the rental market. If you're investing in single lets, that process will be reasonably straightforward, but if you're going for multi-lets it's a lot more refurbishment work and you'll certainly need to be concerned with planning and other local council regulations.

It sounds like a lot of work – and it is – but once you've gone through the process a couple of times, it becomes a lot easier. You know what to look for and your contacts and advisors will get to know exactly what you need from them, so you'll get better leads from agents and a smoother service from your legal and financial people. And if/when you choose to take on an assistant or property manger, you can hand over pretty much all the day-to-day tasks to them and spend your time finding new opportunities – that's the fun part!

The 'passive' investor route

I'm always nervous when I hear people talk about 'passive' investments because it usually means they've invested in a property that's out of their own area on someone else's say-so, often without ever having seen the property or location. It's then tenanted and managed by a third party they've never met and the company offering this supposedly great deal takes a significant fee for their trouble.

I've already talked about investment companies at various points throughout this book and you'll have gathered I'm not keen on them. Some offer a comprehensive portfolio-building service and will not only take an up-front fee and charge you for on-going management, but they may also retain an interest in each property. This supposedly incentivises them to ensure profitability and capital growth but, in reality, between the initial fee and the full management service charge, they're already in profit.

Then you have land banking and overseas opportunities, both of which are even more high risk and less likely to be profitable – indeed, there's a good chance you could come out of the deal worse off than when you went in.

Property sourcers / finders will offer to take the 'hassle' out of securing a good buy to let property and tend to dangle the carrot that they've managed to get it well below what it's worth, which is why you can afford to pay their fee and still be 'in profit'. In reality, these properties are often in less well-off areas and there's a reason they're going cheap! Be very, very wary of anyone offering 'discounted' or 'below market value' deals; there are some out there to be had, but you really need to make sure you do your research on them.

All that being said, there are *some* companies and individuals out there that offer a reasonable service, although I'd still advise you that you'll be better off sourcing your own deals and being in control of the management of your own properties. The time you should spend looking into any third party and checking out their business and track record could be spent analysing your own local market – and that's an investment of time and effort that will continue to reap rewards for you.

If you still think you might like to explore 'hands-off' investing, I'd recommend you take these steps before handing over any money:

1. Choose a company that's recommended by people who have been successful. If you can't get any recommendations, then simply trust your gut on your first impression. Usually it's the companies with the glossiest brochures and the slickest salespeople that are the least likely to make you any real money.
2. Check the company's records with Companies House (companieshouse.gov.uk), where it's free to do a basic search and you can see how long they've been in business,

whether accounts are up to date and whether any forms of the company have gone into liquidation.

3. Visit the head office premises and see if they're really who and what they say they are.

4. Ask to meet the key people behind the business and ask them some questions about what they're offering, the first of which should be, "Are you investing yourself?" If you get the feeling they're not being open and honest, walk away.

5. Grill them about how they arrived at their valuations and projected figures. Importantly, ask whether they're happy for you to send in your own independent surveyor and use your own legal and financial professionals.

Fundamentally, 'armchair' investing can work, but I don't think you should put that little effort into what are probably the biggest investments you'll ever make and have so little control over your financial future. That's why, as I said at the start, property appeals so much to me – because it IS an investment vehicle over which you can have almost complete control.

Consider a mentor

There are numerous pitfalls in this industry. You need to get so many things right and, while you can learn as you go along, it will greatly accelerate your success and you'll be more profitable more quickly if you learn directly form someone who's already done what you're looking to do, made mistakes and worked out how to avoid them, and has investment systems and strategies that are proven to be effective. If you're looking at investing in HMOs, I'd say it's even more important.

A mentor will have an 'open doors' policy on their own property portfolio, showing you what they've achieved and how. They'll come and work with you in your own investment area, helping you get to know the market, and should be there to help you find and negotiate your first deal. They'll guide and advise you on how to build and manage a portfolio and how to achieve the returns you need.

To address the obvious, of course I'm in favour of working with a mentor – that's part of my business. But I wouldn't be doing it if I didn't really think it was worthwhile for my clients and they certainly tell me that mentoring has been hugely beneficial to them. There are testimonials to this effect at the back of this book.

I've also gained a great deal myself from mentoring clients and have even gone into ventures with some of them. This is the one kind of hands-off investment I would recommend you make in property: partnering with someone you have got to know, like and trust, and whose business you've seen inside.

Professional portfolio investors run out of money and mortgage facilities at some point and rely on private investors for capital, so it's well worth asking whether your mentor – or other property professional you might have built a relationship with – whether they'd be interested in investing your money for you. These types of deal are usually uniquely structured, on a case-by-case basis, to ensure that both parties get a return on their investment – you on your financial investment and them on their investment of time and expertise – and can work very well on shorter-term projects, such as new builds, or longer-term investments, such as HMOs.

As I said at the start, there are just so many ways to make money from property, you're bound to find one, or several, that suit you. Take the best advice you can, from people who are experienced in the kind of investing you're considering, and there's no doubt in my mind that property will be able to deliver the future financial security you want.

"Every person who invests in well-selected real estate... adopts the surest and safest method of becoming independent, for real estate is the basis of wealth."

Theodore Roosevelt

KEY STEPS

1. Go through your current pension provision

2. Put together a personal financial statement

3. Meet with a Wealth Manager

4. Identify your business and personal skills

5. Be sure you're happy with the level of risk in property investment and the level of debt you'll incur

6. Consider how much time you're willing and able to put in

7. Discuss with your professional advisor(s) and family the type of investments and level of personal involvement that will best suit you and your goals

8. Research your local market and start building relationships with people in the property industry

9. By all means consider 'passive' investment, but be very wary and carry out thorough due diligence

10. Consider working with a mentor who can accelerate your success and may be able to offer joint-venture opportunities

PART FOUR:

NEXT STEPS…

Even more...
...from Nick Fox Property Mentoring.

Thank you for taking the time to read our book; we hope you've found it helpful. If you'd like to extend your knowledge, please check out our website, where you'll find a wealth of free information and details of our mentoring packages.

We offer a range of mentoring options to suit all needs, from short intensive taster sessions to more comprehensive packages that will give you a deeper understanding of property investment and the buy to let market, focusing on the rewards and implications of building an HMO portfolio.

Various choices available include:

- Half-day 'HMO Education and Tour'
- One-day 'Intensive HMO Property Mentoring Course'
- Two-day 'Intensive HMO Property Mentoring Course'
- 12 months' full access to and support from Nick Fox and his Power Team

Whichever package you choose, you can be assured that Nick's commitment to your personal property goals are absolute. Nick and his team get a real kick out of watching others grow their property portfolios by helping them implement the most successful methods that have been tried and tested over many years.

As skilled and experienced professionals, we present our mentoring sessions in such a way that they're easy to understand, while enabling highly effective learning. The acute insights and practical methodology on offer will help you to take your property business to the next level and secure financial independence for you and your loved ones.

Check out our website **www.nickfox.co.uk** or call us on **01908 930369** to find out more.

Find us on FACEBOOK Nick Fox Mentor TWITTER NickFoxPropertyMentoring
www.nickfox.co.uk EMAIL hello@nickfox.co.uk TEL 01908 930369
NICK FOX PROPERTY MENTORING Suite 150 MK Business Centre
Foxhunter Drive Linford Wood Milton Keynes MK14 6BL

Read on...

Collect the set of books by Nick Fox to help you achieve financial freedom through property investment.

HMO PROPERTY SUCCESS

Do you want a secure financial future that starts sooner, rather than later as you're approaching retirement? By investing in multi-let properties, you can double or even triple the level of rental income generated by single letting, and realise positive cash flow from the start. In this book, multiple business owner and investor, Nick Fox, clearly guides you through the steps to building an HMO portfolio that delivers both on-going income and a tangible pension or lifestyle pot.

ISBN: 978-0-9576516-0-9
RRP: £9.99

THE SECRETS OF BUY TO LET SUCCESS

Are you looking for a sound investment that can give you both income and growth on your capital, but nervous about the future of the property market? This book will put your mind at rest. In The Secrets of Buy to Let Success, Nick Fox shares his knowledge and expertise about the market, guiding the reader step by step through the basics of building a solid and profitable property business - even through an economic crisis. If you're completely new to property investment, this book is a great place to start.

ISBN: 978-0-9927817-2-9
RRP: £9.99

Available now online at
www.amazon.co.uk & www.nickfox.co.uk
Books, iBook, Kindle & Audio

Find us on FACEBOOK Nick Fox Mentor TWITTER NickFoxPropertyMentoring
www.nickfox.co.uk EMAIL hello@nickfox.co.uk TEL 01908 930369

NICK FOX PROPERTY MENTORING Suite 150 MK Business Centre
Foxhunter Drive Linford Wood Milton Keynes MK14 6BL

nickfox
property mentoring

Amazon reviews for HMO Property Success

'A brilliant book'

What sets Nick Fox' book apart from others is the amount of practical detail and advice. It provides a solid and clean framework and a step-by-step guide on how to find, fund, fill and run a profitable house in multiple occupancy. This book has no fluff – it is a very valuable and easy read.

nc3134, 17 Nov 2013

'A MUST read for any HMO owner or investor'

This book is concise, well written, well informed and very practical. I have many other property books but this is by far the best and a must for anyone wanting to invest in HMO property.

Mark MTC, 23 Jan 2014

'Best Property Investment Book'

This no-nonsense approach will guide anyone who is interested in the HMO market into a successful investment; unlike many other publications that purport to be able to help people "get rich quick" with "no money down"; this insightful guide is realistic and proven.

RegSupport, 17 Nov 2013

'Step by step guide to HMO investing'
It is rare in a property book of this kind to find so much solid advice and what must have been hard-earned knowledge - in comparison most other books on the subject provide next to no real information on how to get started. Everyone thinking of getting into hmo property investing should buy this book!

AndyP, 1 Dec 2013

'Great book – especially for those looking to start building a HMO portfolio'
I'm not new to property but am about to start building a HMO portfolio and this book gave me some excellent advice not available in other publications. It also gave me the confidence to proceed down the HMO route!

Stephen Whall, 28 March 2014

Using an easy to understand and simple format, this book is highly effective and informative, neither superficial nor "salesy". A pleasant read for anyone who is time poor and wants to learn HMO property investing.

K Devos, 9 Jan 2014

'Excellent Book'

There are no hard sells, no "get rich" quickly advice, it simply tells you that Nick's investment strategy has proven to give successful results. I strongly advise you to read this book if you are serious about investing.

Elda Breuer, 5 Feb 2014

Testimonials

"I met Nick back in 2013, having been referred through a mutual friend. We hit it off from day one! Nick took me through and explained his entire business: how he had built it up over the years, the ups and downs, and how he had fine-tuned systems and processes to ensure his portfolio and tenants were well managed and producing the correct level of financial return.

I already had a portfolio and a considerable amount of experience in property, having built a substantial letting agency through the 1990s and a property maintenance business in 2003, nevertheless, Nick was still able teach me a great deal.

I was impressed with Nick's openness and honesty. He has very deep knowledge and is without doubt a leading expert in the buy to let property field. Mentor - now business partner and friend."
Richard Leonard, Herts

"Nick and his team are the real deal. Their knowledge and help in moving my investment project forward has been invaluable. Without their expertise I would not have been able to reach my personal property goals or milestones."
Richard Felton, UK

"Nick is a very experienced property professional. His practical advice on setting goals, the pros and cons of this type of investment and how to minimise risks and properly manage a growing portfolio are essential in what can be a very complex investment.

Nick's mentoring is not a get-rich-quick formula but a clear and concise way of demonstrating how a solid property investment strategy can be put into action. And the results are well worth it."
D.Wright, Aberdeen

"Great book, great guy and great results for me after I read 'HMO Property Success'. I've now replaced my job with passive income from HMO properties. Thanks, Nick!"
C.Clark, Bedford

"Nick has clearly got a huge amount of knowledge in his field, and having his support and experience has given me the increased confidence to make my first steps into investing."
Craig Smith, Edinburgh

"I have spent money in the past on various property courses, where you are taught in a group in a classroom, and those have not really helped me. This one-to-one mentoring with Nick was brilliant, as I was actually seeing his business and properties, meeting tenants, getting lots of advice and seeing what worked well and what didn't in a live situation. I have booked another two days

with Nick in my home city next week, to look at various properties and hopefully start my journey as a full-time property investor, and I cannot wait! I highly recommend this type of mentoring!"
James Robinson, Hull

"Both Sarah and I cannot express how much help Nick has been to our property business over the last two years. His support and knowledge have been invaluable. We would thoroughly recommend his mentoring to any budding investor."
Stuart Lewis, Northampton

"Thank you so much for your patience, professionalism and general understanding during our three-day mentoring programme. The visit to see how your office and HMO business runs was incredible and so, so helpful. Without it we would have been at a complete loss. With your guidance and help we have now purchased our first HMO property and look forward to keeping in touch to show you our profitable progress!"
Rebecca Santay-Jones, Harrow

Lightning Source UK Ltd.
Milton Keynes UK
UKOW05f1939061216

289353UK00015B/640/P